*The Silence That Remains*

Ghassan Zaqtan

# THE SILENCE THAT REMAINS

*Selected Poems 1982–2003*

Translated from the Arabic by
**FADY JOUDAH**

Copper Canyon Press
Port Townsend, Washington

Copyright 2017 by Ghassan Zaqtan. Translation copyright 2017 by Fady Joudah.

Printed in the United States of America

Cover art: Mohammed Al Hawajri, *Untitled,* ink on paper, 50 cm × 65 cm, production of 2007 in Gaza

Copper Canyon Press gratefully acknowledges Aissa Deebi for typesetting the Arabic portion of this book.

Copper Canyon Press is in residence at Fort Worden State Park in Port Townsend, Washington, under the auspices of Centrum. Centrum is a gathering place for artists and creative thinkers from around the world, students of all ages and backgrounds, and audiences seeking extraordinary cultural enrichment.

LIBRARY OF CONGRESS CATALOGING-IN-PUBLICATION DATA
Names: Zaqtān, Ghassān, author. | Joudah, Fady, 1971– editor.
Title: The silence that remains : selected poems, 1982–2003 / Ghassān Zaqtān;
    tanslated from the Arabic by Fady Joudah.
Description: Port Townsend, Washington : Copper Canyon Press, [2017] |
    Includes bibliographical references and index.
Identifiers: LCCN 2017004886 (print) | LCCN 2017022705 (ebook) | ISBN
    9781619321755 (ebook) | ISBN 9781556595141 (paperback)
Subjects: | BISAC: POETRY / Middle Eastern.
Classification: LCC PJ7876.A6565 (ebook) | LCC PJ7876.A6565 A2 2017 (print) |
    DDC 892.7/16–dc23
LC record available at https://lccn.loc.gov/2017004886

9 8 7 6 5 4 3 2 FIRST PRINTING

Copper Canyon Press
Post Office Box 271
Port Townsend, Washington 98368

www.coppercanyonpress.org

ACKNOWLEDGMENTS

*A Public Space:* "A Song," "Strangeness (Tiny mirrors released me)"

*Asymptote:* "Children of Palm Trees," "Return," "Song of the Three Patrols," "The Stranger's Song"

*Bennington Review:* "Damascus 1986," "Vehicles in the Dark"

*Granta* online: "Handkerchief"

*Jadaliyya:* "Collective Death," "That Life," "Will They Believe"

*Los Angeles Review of Books:* "Khalil Zaqtan," "Pillow"

*Mantis:* "All of Them," "Bodies on Grass," "Rain," "Sign," "The Lover's Song"

*Modern Poetry in Translation:* "A Swallow," "Conversations with My Father," "Other Conversations"

*Narrative:* "Beyond That," "Other Things," "Three Stones"

*Plume:* "A Woman in Damascus That Year," "While She Was Sleeping in Baghdad"

*Poem:* "Had You Slept beside Me," "Happy with My Things"

*The Adroit Journal:* "Glee"

*The Times Literary Supplement:* "All of Them," "The Lover's Song"

*World Literature Today:* "Old Reasons (Old friend, when we meet)"

The foreword to the book first appeared in the Los Angeles Review of Books online under the title: "The Silence That Remains: On Translating the Poetry of Ghassan Zaqtan."

# Contents

from *The Heroism of Things*

from *Biography in Charcoal*

## Foreword

Once we see in the need to "translate" the obvious need to "betray,"
we shall see the temptation to betray as something desirable, comparable perhaps to erotic exaltation. Anyone who hasn't experienced the ecstasy of betrayal knows nothing about ecstasy at all.

JEAN GENET

As I completed my work on Ghassan Zaqtan's recent poetry in *Like a Straw Bird It Follows Me,* I wanted to read more of his earlier poems. I asked him to send me copies of those collections but that proved to be a story. At first, he sent me a copy of *Putting Description in Order,* his 1998 volume of new and selected poems. The book featured work from four previous collections. It began with *Old Reasons* (1982) — the poet's third collection, which he considers his actual debut — and concluded with new pieces meant to announce a forthcoming project, *Zodiac of the Horse,* which never materialized.

The copy of *Description* appeared to have spent much time in sweaty hands or been stored in damp conditions on a forgotten shelf. Just as its title promised, *Description* was the first exhibit, one can say, in how Zaqtan rearranged his art: not simply a matter of choosing the best from the past, but also of disassembling the original body (its sequence mostly) that housed many of the poems, and then reconstructing a new corpus for them.

The second exhibit was also performed on the body of *Description.* With black pen, Zaqtan had marked some of the pages of my copy. Mostly he edited punctuation, crossed out a few poems, and tinkered with a couple of titles or some stanza breaks. The most intriguing intervention, however, was his occasional deletion of a section in a sequence or a stanza in a poem. He seemed carefree. He was quoting and misquoting himself, reshaping and reforming memory.

I took note of this precedent — Zaqtan's aesthetic of nonchalance, illusory and paradoxical as it may be, regarding his own text's iteration. It excited me to work with a poet who protects his margins' rights to wander. It's a feeling I know well. Borderlands become central, all boundaries active. The record is no holier than the self.

What were the early poems like when experienced within their "original" homes? What of the poems Zaqtan didn't include in the "selected" works? I turned away from *Description* and asked for the early books whole, all four of them, but Zaqtan told me that copies were hard to come by or part with, especially *Old Reasons*. And in the case of *Not for My Sake* (1992), Zaqtan could obtain only a copy of the bound galleys.

*Old Reasons,* it turns out, had narrowly escaped erasure. Its publication preceded the Israeli invasion of Lebanon in 1982 by a few days. Zaqtan possessed fifteen author copies and held on to them in his apartment in Beirut. On the first day of the invasion, an Israeli rocket lodged itself in the third floor, where he lived, and burned the books and everything else. Luckily Zaqtan had left the building earlier. On his person were two copies that he intended to give to friends. The publisher had distributed no more than a hundred copies before the rest of them burned in their boxes in the warehouse. Years rolled by and copies of *Old Reasons* began to resurface and reunite with their author in unexpected places — in Damascus or Algiers, for example. They were the copies that the publisher had managed to send out before incineration became the fate of the remainder.

Was this another level of deletion (and its ghosts) that might explain Ghassan Zaqtan's art and his relation to it?

In the epigraph to his landmark collection, *The Heroism of Things* (1988), Zaqtan wrote: "I'm mystified / how do I / rearrange the poem / everything's been said." This "everything" is, of course, what others have said — a history of documented speech, local and otherwise. It is what the poet himself had begun to say in previous work, what he hears the previous work speak back to him constantly. And yet it is something more, a rehearsal and iteration of silence. Here is the title poem from *Not for My Sake*:

> Not for my sake
> or yours
> and not for the sake of what others had agreed to describe
>     and fully did
> speech and its loads
> are not mine
> before me
>     all of it was

Even today this preoccupation, this waiting and listening (and retrieving), is palpable in his work. "Three Hallways," the only remaining poem from *Zodiac of the Horse,* found its way into Zaqtan's most recent collection, *Marchers Call Out to Their Brothers.* The title comes from a line in the 1998 poem and is difficult to capture in translation. They're not pedestrians in protest or demonstration, not amblers through a park, not a file of soldiers. They are the dispossessed, the displaced and dispersed, on foot.

✤

If the narrative of human consciousness has already been told countless times over countless reproducible nights, then perhaps what remains is the private memory that haunts a mind. To have memory and to articulate memory are two different things. The memory recalled in silence seems always whole (in the company of its entourage of feeling), or at least far more complete than when articulation is attempted. As time proceeds or recurs, gaps appear in the memory previously articulated. The more one attempts to capture memory and enunciate it, the more one is resigned to an endless task.

Perhaps then, in rearranging memory, Zaqtan views his past work as a painting long unexhibited, which now seems unfinished. And so he takes the canvas out of storage and applies minor, subtle brushstrokes to it, as if he were his own art's historian. His views on the subject are clear in "Always":

> Seven days ago
> was Thursday afternoon
> I read the poem
> the one that was supposed to have been finished
> that morning
> and it wasn't finished
>
> For seven years
> I finish it every morning then doze off
> and by evening
> I always catch it
> opening its doors on the sly
> and calling talk in

Throughout Zaqtan's work, recurrence comes bearing new gifts. Childhood, friends, marriage, eros, and death, in their various forms, suggest an obsessive irresolution, as if what is incompletely remembered is betrayed. And since memory itself is oriented toward the future (a life carried forth), the betrayal never ceases. Enthralled, circuitous, and unrelenting tenderness drives Zaqtan's poetry and propagates it.

❋

The aesthetic of fragment as the art of the fragile: an imaginative archaeology that became powerfully manifest when we had to deal with the logistics of this bilingual edition.

At the time of this writing, Zaqtan's early books are scheduled for republication in Arabic in 2017. In preparation, the poet again took up his subtle pen to copyedit the older works. The erratic, sometimes intoxicated and painterly punctuation of the early versions (which served as my template for these translations) is significantly streamlined, normalized. Indentations disappear, and infrequently words and minor phrases are replaced. Some poems changed their form slightly. And in a couple of instances the form was radically altered so that I had to request a return to origin, so to speak, for the sake of this production.

My translation evolved from its original template and was finished before I received the new Arabic files of the older poems for this bilingual edition. I made no further alterations. My work, then, adheres to neither mirror, inhabiting an in-between space where silences are performed. A genome's dance with its phenotype: the result simultaneously questions and affirms fidelity or filiation. The possibility for rereading (and thus rewriting) a text, for both poet and translator, expands.

This offers something new, unintended, divergent to the reflexive approach to bilingual works of art. They are not reliable as tool for learning a language, are not necessarily limited to the accuracy of the looking glass. Zaqtan and I, with our editor Michael Wiegers's support, agreed to let the life of the work be apparent — uncorrected, so to speak, by what would betray the silences it generates.

❋

What then of the silence this book speaks of: the "silence" that I lifted out of the poem Ghassan Zaqtan wrote as an elegy for his father and which bears his name, "Khalil Zaqtan"?

When a reader traverses where a writer disappears, the former can more easily see and hear the latter's silences. A reader can trace the father's presence in "Abu Zuhair" and in "Also the House" and there are many other figures that perform this kind of ghostly materialization in Zaqtan's poems. The mother, especially in "Three Hallways," is a favorite of mine. But, beyond theme, place and its protagonists, and the doubles and cameos of objects and persons that populate the poems, there are also the silences of the lyric in Zaqtan's poems, the energy fields of multiple dictions and registers.

"Old Reasons (Old friend, when we meet)" returns in its narrative intensity to "Also the House" or "Another Death." "Rain" becomes "Pillow" or "Things That Don't Happen." Eros persists ecstatic with psyche. To read and live with the poems is to notice how the silences morph. Across Zaqtan's poems silences inhabit syntax, translocate within and alter it. Sentences shed meaning and lyric shifts to ordinary speech.

Language as a moving object: perhaps in reading literature, we come closest to experiencing a life, ours and another's, in multidimensional space.

❇

No silence is alone. Each silence is two. One is expressible, lends itself to speech, and the other is ineffable. That is what Ibn Arabi described as the two silences: the silence of the tongue and the silence of the heart. Only the former can be formulated, and "whether you keep silent or make an utterance, you speak." And yet "between utterance and silence," between articulation and its antithesis, al-Nifarri said, "there's a liminal zone wherein lies the mind's grave and the graves of things." This is the threshold that propels our silences toward their corporeal conditions.

All silence is resistance, perhaps immanence. If silence is sacred language, golden, then everything else is inferior translation. The silence that lends itself to the translation of its feeling is what we find, or imagine we find, between the words, between the lines. If one is compelled to translate the feeling of silence, one enters history. We are instead urged to "create silence," as Kierkegaard wrote, to reclaim and reenter it: a silence, as antidote to white noise, seems least corruptible (or most antinomian) in an irrevocably chronological world.

I believe that of silence something always remains, unexpressed, inexpressible. The silences in this book are as universal and collective as they are individual and singular. Silence here is Palestinian silence.

❇

How does one write Palestinian silence into English? The question demands silence. The answer — a translation at best — demands a willingness to receive and accept.

To reverberate Derrida's echo of the wound of silence that, once spoken, opens into history, I can descend — briefly — into the history of the Palestinian question. Ghassan Zaqtan's father, mother, and extended family were expelled from their homes and lands in Zakariya in 1948 at the hands of Israeli forces. Zaqtan was born a refugee in 1954 in Beit Jala in the West Bank and grew up east of the River Jordan in Karameh refugee camp, which Israel also razed to the ground in 1968. The family had to move elsewhere in Jordan, to Russeifa and Amman.

In his twenties Ghassan Zaqtan joined the Palestinian revolution. Eventually he took up residence in Lebanon. And from there a life of exile ("wherever we are is ours") until Zaqtan's return to Ramallah in 1994. This timetable is evident in his oeuvre, and it is perhaps most visible in *Biography in Charcoal* (2003) where, in the spirit of Cavafy, Zaqtan sketches out his dislocation.

✿

What is beautiful, liberating, and daring here is the mention of the Palestinian revolution. Describing a Palestinian of that time as belonging to the revolution is redundant. The whole of Palestinian society, in its myriad forms and locations, was engaged. Ghassan Zaqtan's early works, especially the first four collections in this *Silence,* give form to those days and what birthed them. To speak of the poems' nuance, to give them historical utterance — in "Migration," for example, in "Collective Death," or in "Will They Believe," in "Handkerchief" and "Conversations with My Father" — betrays the silence of poetry. Even to a Palestinian who might engage the explicatory or revelatory, this silence remains indescribable in some way. Comfort, sorrow, rapture — as forms of knowing — shadow the ineffable.

Take, for example, the "Three Stones" (whose later cameo in a brief line in "Also the House" tells us of their place at the front door). The poem comes from *Old Reasons* and begins a short sequence (originally titled "Stones for Fathers and Us"). The "three steps" become the only silence that remains of that sequence:

> Three stone steps
> where our fathers sit
> in their full gear

looking as mean
as we knew them to be
and as they didn't wish to be
not even for a day

How does one carry this within for generations and across languages? And yet who among us has not? Another moment is found in "The Death of the Artillery Youth." Are we able to read the Promethean in it? Who holds fire as gift and who holds it as destruction, and at which coordinates in time?

✳

Or perhaps I offer this. *The Silence That Remains* is a necessary companion to Jean Genet's masterful last work, *Prisoner of Love.* The young artist who Zaqtan was, when he lived those Palestinian days in Genet's book, is a mirror image to an outcast like Genet, and to the visionary rebellion and betrayal that Genet achieves in memory, praise, and elegy of the Palestinian revolution. Here's Genet in the opening pages of his book:

> Was the Palestinian revolution really written on the void, an artifice super-imposed on nothingness, and is the white page, and every little blank space between the words, more real than the black characters themselves? Reading between the lines is a level art; reading between the words a precipitous one. If the reality of time spent among — not with — the Palestinians resided any-where, it would survive between all the words that claim to give an account of it. They claim to give an account of it, but in fact it buries itself, slots itself exactly into the spaces, recorded there rather than in the words that serve only to blot it out. Another way of putting it: the space between the words contains more reality than does the time it takes to read them. [. . .]
>
> So did I fail to understand the Palestinian revolution? Yes, completely. [. . .] The reality lay in involvement, fertile in hate and love; in people's daily lives; in silence, like translucency, punctuated by words and phrases.

Genet "among — not with — the Palestinians" was twice an outsider. To be fully present in the Palestinian revolution and not be totally of it, he sought proof that the Palestinian revolution not only existed but also was spectacular. He waited for silences to return to him before they could take shape on the page. For Ghassan Zaqtan there is a different agency, urgency, and intimacy of language and body:

> Happy and thrilled with my voice as it resembles me,
> as it calms down when I'm crying or in longing,

as it puts on its old clothes . . . as I hug you,
as it walks out of me barefoot in the night
to arrange itself for the alphabet
of your sleep

Whatever its domain of consciousness, Palestinian silence is here, "oppressed, beloved, exposed / and full of perishing radiance" — "banners that tug / only at trees // and are not retrieved / a triumph." Ecstasy pervades the book. Survival, remembrance, desire, resolve: to be "together, alone, in the poem."

Fady Joudah, 2017

Note: The quotation of Jean Genet comes from *Prisoner of Love*, translated from the French by Barbara Bray.

*The Silence That Remains*

from

*Old Reasons*

1982

# الأَحاديث

«إلى خليل زقطان في «الرصيفة» القريبة من «عمّان».

– ١ –

قال لي :
حجرٌ في الطريق
لهُ ضفّتاهُ
الرمالُ الفسيحةُ
والخضرةُ المستريحة
لكنه حجرٌ واحد
في طريقٍ.

قال لي :
ليس غير انفعالي معي
ناشراً أضلعي
للوهادِ الفقيرةِ حول القرى،
للقرى
إذْ تُمسّي عليها التلالُ
مساءَ التهاني
وإذْ يهبط القصفُ
إذ يصبح الصخرُ
ما دَوّرَتْهُ الرِّيَاحُ
وما أنبتتهُ الأصابعْ.

قال لي :
ما أن أفقتُ
وما أن وقفتُ
وما أن تبيّنتُ جسمي من الكائنات
وميّزتُ صوتي
حتى استفاقت جروحُ اليدين
وحتى رأتني الكمائن
واشتدَّ صوتُ السلاحْ.

قال لي :

*Conversations with My Father*


He said to me:
A stone on the road
has its shores
its span
of sand and tranquil greenery
but it's one stone
on a road

He said:
I was alone my reaction and I
hanging
my ribs on the impoverished valleys
around the villages
when darkness greets them at evening,
a congratulatory evening,
and bombardment descends
and rocks become
what the wind rounds
and what fingers bud

He said to me:
As soon as I woke
and stood up and could tell my body
from the creatures around me
and discern my voice,
the wounds in my hands became conscious,
the ambush spotted me,
gunfire intensified

He said:
Like a land that gathers its regions
before the fighter planes pass overhead:
will the land succeed
or will the jets?

مثلِّ أرض تلمُّ    أقاليمها
قبلَ أن تعبرَ الطائرات
فهل تنجح الأرضُ
أم تنجح الطائرات؟.

# غرابة

أطلقتني المرايا الصغيرة
في كفِّ أمّي
وأطلقني القشُّ
في سطح منزلنا
وأطلقتُ نفسي إليكَ.
فانتبه جيداً،
أنت تكسرني في يديكَ.
وانتبه
إذ تشدُّ على قفص الصدر
أو مفصلٍ فائرٍ في الذراعْ
انَّ عظميَ هشٌّ
وأغنيتي تطحنُ الصخرَ.

*Strangeness*


Tiny mirrors released me into my mother's palms
hay released me to the roof of our house
and I released myself to you
be careful!
you're breaking me
with your hands
be careful
when you squeeze my ribs
or press a lax
joint in my arm
my bones
are frail
my song
grinds stone

## الأَحَادِيث

زهرةٌ من مساء الأحدّ
زهرةٌ للحصانَ الجميلِ
من مساء سيسقطُ خلفَ العمارات
فور ابتعادي عن النافذة.


مَضَى زمنٌ
منذ خرّبَشتُ اسماً على مقعدي المدرسيّ.
مَضَى زمنٌ
منذ أورقتُ مثل النبات الخرايِّ
يِّ الحارة الشركسيّة.
مضى زمنٌ
منذ عينيّ «رندا»
مضى زمنٌ هائلٌ منذ «رندا».


مضى زمن
منذ أطلقتُ قلبي
فحطَّ على شرفة السيدة.
أنت يا وردةَ الزمهريرّ
أنتَ يا سيّدة
أنت يا حلّةَ الوصف
ردِّيَ لقلبي جدائلَهُ
كي يطيرَ.


دخلَ المساءُ حقولَ قلبي
وارتدى نخلاً
وباباً عالياً
وفضاءً
أعدّ لي حنطتي ويديّ
أعدّ لي أوّل الكلماتّ
فإنّي واحدٌ يِّ الليل
مستترٌ ببَرْد الليلِ
ملتفّ ببَرَد الليلِ
مُستوفى
وقد دخلّ المساءُ عليّ.

*Other Conversations*


A Sunday evening flower for the beautiful horse,
an evening that will fall behind the buildings
once I step away from the window

A long time has passed
since I carved my name on the school chair

a long time has passed
since I leafed like a mythical plant
in the Circassian neighborhood,
a hell of a long time
since Randa's eyes

And since I released my heart to alight
on a Russian woman's veranda:
Frost flower, description's garnish,
give back to my heart its braids so it can fly

The evening entered my fields wearing
palm trees, my first henna and my first words,
then wrapped me in its cold and left me
fulfilled . . .
but if our pigeons lose their way
give back to me what stone did say:

A long time has passed
since the travel that travel tossed
in our feet

The blond Russian once read
my father's name in a poetry book,
she used to read me and shut
her eyes as if warm snow
were coming through the window

يا خوفي
إذا تاهت يمامتنا
يا خوفي على قلبي
سينكسرُ
أعدْ لي ما روى الحجرُ
مضى زمنٌ
على السفر الذي
ألقاهُ في أقدامنا السفرُ.

كانت الروسيةُ الشقراءُ
تقرأ في كتاب الشعر
اسمَ أبي
وتقرأني
وتغمضُ قلبها حيناً
فأشعرُ أنَّ ثلجاً دافئاً
يأتي من الشبّاك.

أقطفُ وردةً من أينْ
كي أُهدي لها ورداً
وأدخلُ في رداءِ الثلجّ.

مضى زمن
منذ ألقت طيور الحساسين
فصل الشتاء على السقف
وارتفعت في الشتاء
وفي السقف أفعى
و«بوص» تلاصق في البرد حتى انحنى
وفي السقف «دلف» من الانحناء
وفوقَ الترابِ الملبَّد وجهانِ
وجهي
ووجه أبي في الإناءْ
أعدْ لي زهرةَ الحنّاءْ
أعَدْ لي
زهرةَ الحنّاءْ
أعدّ لي
زهرةَ
الحنّاءْ.

Where in this snow can I pick a rose for her
where can I wear snow's dress?

A long time has passed
since the swallows dropped winter
on the roof and a snake
climbed the wall and plaster held
and a plank in the ceiling bent
and two faces
over the padded dirt
were mine
and my father's in the jug

Father
give me back
the henna flower
give me back
the henna flower

and Mother,
as you wear
your late-night prayers,
give them back their night:

The absentee always returns
horses to their kin

ويا أُمُّ
ما شرّدتني المدائنُ
إنّي أُشرِّدها في دمي
وأتركها عرضةً لارتحالي
وزنبقةً في ذراع القتيلِ.

ويا أُمُّ
إذ تتعبين النوافل في آخر الليلِ
ردّي لها ليلها
إن من غابَ
إذ غابَ
ردَّ الجيادَ إلى أهلها.

غرابة

نهارٌ وأمضي
وأطلقُ اسمي على كلِّ شيء
وأتركهُ لامعاً في سِياجٍ بعيدٌ .

نهارٌ سألقيه من سلّتي
ثمَّ يأتي صغارٌ
يَلمُّونهُ من تراب الحقولِ
ومن قنوات المياه
وزيتِ المكائنْ .

ولو ينحني النخلُ
لانشقَّ قلبي
وقَبَّلْتهُ ألفَ قُبْلَة
ولكنهُ النخلُ عالٍ
ومنديلُ أُمّي علىً كفّها .

*Strangeness*


A day then I'll go,
call everything by my name
and leave it glistening on a distant fence

A day I'll toss out of my basket
before kids come and gather it
from the dirt of the fields,
irrigation channels
and engine oil

If only the palm trees would bend
my heart would split
and I would kiss it a thousand times

but the palm trees are high
and my mother is holding
her handkerchief

أشياءُ أُخرى

مساءٌ وحيد
ونافذةٌ واحدة
إناءُ الزهور على المائدة
زهرةٌ ذَبُلَت
أو تكادُ
هذه أنت.

أَلَمْ تنتبه بعدُ
أنّا الوحيدين
ﻲﻓ غفلةٍ من هزيعٍ أخيرّ.

أَلَمْ تنتبه بعدُ
أنّا كسرنا الزجاجَ
وأنّ الذي لاحَ خلفَ الخطى
إذْ ركضنا معاً
معطفي
عالقاً ﻲﻓ السياجْ.

الذي باعني
مُسدّساً مُهرّباً
باعني
ذخيرةً مُهرّبة.

والذي زارني
ﻲﻓ مساءِ الأحدْ
لم يعُدْ.

فاهدئي زوجتي
اهدئي
حينَ أتلو النشيدْ
وأُطلقُ طيراً من القلب
طيراً وحيداً
لشخصٍ وحيدْ.

*Other Things*


A lonely evening
and an only window,
the flower vase is on the table,
a flower has wilted
                    or is almost there
that's you

Haven't you noticed
we're the only two
oblivious to the end of the night?
Haven't you noticed
that we broke the glass
                    and the one
who appeared after our running
was my coat
caught in the fence?

The one who sold me
a smuggled gun
                    sold me
smuggled bullets
and the one who paid me
a visit on Sunday night
hasn't returned

Dear wife calm down
                    calm down
as I recite a song
and release a bird in the heart
a lonely bird
to a lonely one

# مطر

دخلنا إلى لغة الغيم
فانتشرَ الطقسُ
هَلْ تفتحينَ المظلّة
أَمْ تُغلقينَ المطرْ؟

وما كانَ في يدنا غير ألعابِ أطفالنا.

*Rain*

We have entered the language of clouds
the weather is all over
will you open your umbrella
or turn off the rain?

We only held our children's toys in our hands

وإذْ نلتقي أيُّها الصديق
رفّان من الأجنحة
وسنوات من القسوة
ومخيّلة واحدة،
لن نتبادل الأنخاب
إذْ لن يكون هناك من يعصرُ خمراً
للأعيادِ القديمة.

الأقدام التي هدرتْ خلفَ البيوت
وأنصتنا لها واجفين
كانت أقداماً فقط
تهدر خلف البيوت.

النساءُ اللواتي أثرنَ بهجةَ العشب
وسائقَ العربة
وبغلَ الحراثة
وأحواضَ الخضار،
تركنَ على الترابِ السميك
خبزَ الأزواج
ومقصّات العمل
والأصابع الخشنة
وغادرنَ إلى ريفٍ بعيد.

رجلٌ وحيدٌ
يُطيّر عصافيراً
ويشربُ نخبَ الأرض المنخفضة
والسّلالة الغارقة في السمرة والوهم،
كأسهُ الممزوج بترابِ الأغاني.

امرأةٌ ناضرة الطرف
ومبتعدةٌ عن زينتها
شهقتْ طويلاً خلفَ العجلاتِ
وظهر العربة.

*Old Reasons*


Old friend, when we meet, we will meet
as two shelves of wings and many harsh years,
as one imagination that won't exchange toasts:
there's no one to stomp the grapes for the ancient feasts

The footsteps that rumbled behind the houses,
to which we listened frightened,
were only footsteps rumbling
behind the houses

The women who kindled the elation of grass,
the coachman, the plow mule,
and vegetable pots, those women
left behind on the thick soil
their husbands' bread, scissors, and sickles
and their own rough fingers
then departed to a distant countryside

The lonely man,
who flew sparrows
and drank the toast of lowlands and lineage,
drowned in delusion and late nights,
his glass mixed with the dust of songs

The young, voluptuous woman
who was disinterested in her makeup
let out a long sigh

as the bikes and carriages passed
as a cloud sloped down toward some darkening lead
in the fired-up southern peaks, she gathered
her bundle on her back and slowly
the morning dew crept into her spine

وإذْ انحدَرتْ سحابة
نحوَ رصاص داكن
في القمم الهَائجةً جنوباً
جمعت أطراف الحزمة إلى ظهرها
ورويداً
تسرّبَ البللُ الصباحي إلى سلسلةِ الظهر
وحيثُ الآلهة
ارتعشتْ قبّةُ البدن
وسقط مطرٌ لم تعرفهُ الخلائق.


رمّانة القلب
التي فلقناها ذاتَ صيف،
تزوّجها الدوريُّ المنافس
البطيء في طيرانه
الذي لا يملكُ ريشاً جميلاً لنحسده
أو تاجاً على الرأسَ
لنحاولَ اصطياده.


المعادن
المعادنُ تتدحرجُ
تصفرُّ وتعوي
وتأتلق في فَضاء الهُوّة.
ووسطَ الهدير
في تلكَ الزاوية بالضبطِ
من نافذة البنِّ في مقلتيكَ
يلمعُ رنينَ المعدنِ
ويهدرُ الرّعدُ
جرسُ الآلهة القديمُ.
ثمّ وجدنا قمصاننا
مشدودةً إلى سهامِ الأعداء.

And where the gods were the body was
packed with goose bumps, and a rain
that creatures had never known the likes of
fell down

The heart's pomegranate
that we split open that summer
married the rival house sparrow
whose feathers weren't beautiful enough
for us to envy

And anyway
he was slow in his flight
and had no crest
for us to hunt

The metal
the metal that tumbled
and whistled and howled
and sparkled in the space of the abyss
and in the middle of the roar
exactly there, in that corner
where coffee windows used to open in your eyelids

That metal gleamed and rang
and thundered, that old bell of the gods

That was when we found our shirts taut
toward the enemies' arrows

حجارة للآباء

ثلاثُ درجات من الحجرِ
عليها يجلسُ الآباءُ
بكامل عدّتهم،
قساةً كما عهدناهم
وكما لم يُريدوا في أيِّ يوم.

*Three Stones*


Three stone steps
where our fathers sit
in their full gear
looking as mean
as we knew them to be
and as they didn't wish to be
not even for a day

أسباب قديمة

بلا مرح الأب
وبلا مبَخرة الأُمّ
وبلا نخلة الأَجداد المهزوزة دائماً
إلى الأتقيَاء
بعيداً عن الجري
على حواف المياه الثقيلة
وصياح الصَبية
وهم ينفلون أعشاشَ العصافير
ويكسّرونَ البيض
ويرتجفون من «الملاريا»
ومرارة «الكينيا»
بعيداً عن أرواح القتلى الطوّافة
حولَ برك الأولِياء
بعيداً عن أملاك العائلة
وحيداً
وموحشاً
وخاوياً
ومنزوعا من الأسئلة.

*Old Reasons*

Without the father's mirth
without the mother's incense
or the grandfather's palm tree
that is always shaken
toward the pious
and with no running
by the edges of heavy current
no shouting of kids
who ruffle bird nests
break eggs
tremble from malaria
and quinine's bitterness
and away
from the souls of the dead
who hover around the ponds of saints
and away from family property
alone
forlorn
empty
and stripped of questions

سنونو

ربما جاءَ من فجوةٍ
يۓ جدار المساء
حَبَا مثلَ طفلٍ
ولمّا انتبهتُ علَى حَبْوه
صارَ سجّادةً للقصيدةَ.
ربما كان اسماً
وما زاد عن كونه
أحرفاً يۓ مدارٍ.


كأنَّ السنونو
ابتعادٌ عن الأرضِ
يرجُمنا بالمياه
ويتلو علينا السُوَرْ.


كأنّا معاً
كأنّا «هناك» مع الميّتين الذين «هناك»
كأنّ «هناك»
قريبٌ كما لم نعوّد أصابعنا
أن ترى
والقرى
ليتها لم تكنّ.

*A Swallow*


Maybe he came out of a hole
in the evening's wall
crawling like a child
and when I noticed him crawl
he became a carpet for the poem

Maybe he was a name
that did not exceed his being
a bunch of letters in an orbit

As if a swallow
is moving away from the earth
he hurls water at us and reads us scriptures

As if we were together
as if we had been there
with the dead who are there
as if over there

is as close as our habit
of not coaching our fingers to see
. . . and the villages
. . . wish they never were

## مكان آخر

لن يتذكّرها أحد
ولن يتوقّف في بابها مسافر.

ستغلق حوانيتها
وتخرّب بيوتها الكبيرة
وتهرم نساؤها
وسيأتي الجراد من جهاتها الأربع
يقرضها كما يقرض خسّة في حقل.
وإذ ذاك
لن يسقطَ عليها مطر السماء،
فلا فائدة
من يزرع في الصخر
ومن يتذكر،
وحدهُ
القابع في سجنها
كوسادةِ الحجر.

## Another Place

No one will remember her
no traveler will stand in her door
she will close her pubs and her mansions
will become ruins
her women will age
and from four corners locusts will descend
and gnaw her
as they gnaw lettuce in a field

If that happens
no rain will come from the sky
no point!
      who will farm in rock?
who'll remember?
Only the one
squatting in her prison
like a pillow of stone

سيرة

أُمّي فلّاحةٌ لا تؤمن بالتعاويذ
وأبي امتنعّ عن الكتابةِ
وواصلَ التدخين
حتى مات
وأنا
اقتفيتُ المناشيرَ السريّة
حتى وصلتُ إلى «الفاكهاني».

*Biography*

My mother is a peasant who doesn't believe
in charms and amulets,
my father quit writing
but not smoking
until he died
and I
tracked secret leaflets
that led me to headquarters

أغنية

المجدُ الذي وُزِّعَ بالتساوي
على الجميع :
أوسمةً للقادة
ومدائحَ للرتب الصغيرة
وصوراً للقتلى.
أنهى دورتهُ واستندَ على أكياسِ الرملْ
ولكَ الآن
أن تُدخِّنَ لفافة بكاملها
بانتظار الحربِ القادمة.

*A Song*

The glory that has been evenly split
among everyone
into medals for the leaders
praise for rank and file
and pictures for the dead
has finished its cycle
and is leaning now
on sandbags so you can roll
and smoke your whole
tobacco pack
before the next war comes

from

*Banners*

1984

## هجرة

كيفَ أنّ الرجالَ مضُوا .. كلّهم
دونَ أن يتركوا قَشّةً كي ننام،
دونَ أن يتركوا
ولداً «يـ الحراسة»
قلماً للكتابة
فحماً لهذا البقاء المخيف !

كيف أنّ الرجال مضوا ... كلّهم
دونَ أن يتركوا
سلّةً كي نلمَّ بها الفطرَ
قبّعة كي نخبّئ شيبَ الهموم
يداً كي نصافحَ
أو حكمةً نستعين بها
غير حكمتهم يـ الرحيل !

كيف أنَّ الرجالَ مضوا كلّهم.

خطٌّ من القبّعات القصيرة
خطٌّ من الأحذيةَ
وقشٌّ على وبرِ الصوف.

## Migration

How the men went . . . all of them,
without leaving a straw for our sleep,
without leaving a boy "on watch,"
a pen for writing
or coal for this frightening survival

How the men went . . . all of them,
without leaving us
a basket for gathering mushrooms,
a hat to hide our gray worries,
a hand to shake
or a wisdom to aid us
besides their wisdom of departure

How they all went
a row of small caps
a line of shoes
hay stuck to fluffy wool

## إشارة

غيّرتنا المدنُ
غيّرتنا المصاعد
مالتْ بنا الطرقُ المائلة.
غيّرتنا «العماراتُ» إذ سرقت
من شبابيكنا
ـ دون أن نعترض ـ
ركض أولادنا في فضاء السنة.
غيّرتنا الصحافةُ
والغرفُ الضيّقة.
غيّرتنا أحاديثنا ..
والأغاني التي تعصرُ القلبَ
حتى انتهينا إلى هذه الشرنقة.

*Sign*


Cities changed us
elevators changed us
the slanted roads swung us about,
the high-rises that stole from our windows
our children's running in the space
of a year (and we didn't object)
also changed us,
journalism changed us
and the narrow small rooms
our conversations
and the songs that wrung the heart
until we ended up here
in this chrysalis

# يوم هادئ

لا قتلى على الطرقاتِ
يومٌ هادئ
والسيرُ عاديٌّ
وثمة فسحة لنشيّع القتلى الذين
مضوا نهارَ الأمسّ.

ثمة فسحة لنضيفَ
حلماً، فكرةً، ولداً صغيراً
دفعةً للزورق المحروسِ
اسماً للخليّة
وردةً لحبيبةٍ أخرى
يداً لرفيق.

ثمة فسحة لنظلّ أحياء لبعض الوقت
تكفي كي أهزَّ يديك
تكفي كي نطال الشمسّ.

يومٌ هادئ يمشي على قدميهِ في بيروت
يرقصُ في الطريق،
يُعيقُ سيرَ الحافلاتِ برقصه،
لا يشتري صحفاً ولا يتذكّرُ الموتى
ـ مضت صحف الصباح إلى المكاتب
واستراح الميّتون على رصيفِ «مقابر الشهداء»
في أطراف «صبرا» . .

يومٌ هادئ
والسيرُ عاديّ
وجارتنا ستخرج في قميص النوم
تنشرُ بيننا نعساً وصحواً فاتراً،
وتهمُّ أن تحكي
فتكسل أن تلمَّ الحرف
ـ أين يكون في هذا الصباحِ الشّاسعِ المغترّ !

## Calm Day

No dead on the streets today
is a calm day,
traffic is normal,
there's ample room for the procession
of yesterday's dead,
room to add
> a dream, an idea, a little boy,
> an extra push for the beloved boat,
> a nom de guerre for the cell,
> a rose for a new love,
> a hand to a comrade

Some room to stay alive for some time,
enough time to shake your hands
and reach the sun

Today is a calm day, a pedestrian day
in Beirut dancing in the streets,
obstructing buses and not buying
newspapers:
> the newspapers already went out to offices
and the dead are resting on the Pavement of Martyrs
at the outskirts of Sabra

A calm day,
our neighbor will step out in her nightgown
to hang some sleepiness around us,
some sluggish waking
she's too lethargic to gather letters into words

Where is life on this vast sauntering morning?
We won't leave

لن نمضي
سيأتي من بياض قميصها سبب
ليحملنا إلى الطرقات
قتلى في «صباح الخيرُ».

Out of the whiteness of her gown a reason
will come to carry us down to the streets
dead in her "Good morning"

# مرور

في فسحة التقاطع الأخيرْ
في اللحظةَ الأخيرة
التي يُضيئُها اللّهبْ،
حديقةٌ لحارس عجوز
الوقتُ في يديهَ نحلة
تفرُّ خلسةً وتكسرُ السببْ،
والصدفةُ التي لم تعترض خفوتُه
تلمُّ جمرها الأخيرْ.
وإذْ أمرُّ ـ بعد غارتين ـ متعباً
أشدُّ من غلالة الحديث : مرحبا ...
سينحني كزنبقة
ويرقصُ الفراشُ
حول سنِّهِ الذهبْ.

*Passing*


In the opening of the last intersection
in the last moment that flames illuminate
there's a garden for an old watchman
who holds time in his hands as a bee
that furtively flees and fractures
cause
       The coincidence
that didn't interject his watch
gathers its final embers as I pass
exhausted after two raids
gripping my gauzy speech:
Hello . . .
He bows like an iris
and butterflies dance around
his golden tooth

## ينبغي أن تقف

قبلَ أنْ تدخلَ «الفاكهاني» الصغير
قبلَ أن تتعطفْ
قبلَ «صبرا» «بزاروبة» واحدة
ينبغي أن تقف.
ثمةَ امرأة ـ نحلة ـ بين تلكَ السقوفْ
ثمةَ امرأة ـ راية ـ لا تُرى من بعيد
سوف تأتيك بالخبزِ والماء والأسئلة
سوف يأتيك من وجهها شاعرٌ ذاهلٌ
لم يفكّر بأعماله الكاملة.
قبل أن تدخلَ «اَلفاكهاني» الصغيرُ
ينبغي أن تقفْ
ينبغي أن تطيلَ الوقوفْ.

## You Must Pause

Before you enter that neighborhood
and turn the corner one slither of an alley
just before the refugee camp,
you must pause

There's a woman a bee among those roofs,
a woman a banner that can't be seen
from a distance, she will come to you
with bread and water and questions

And from her face a dumbfounded poet
who's yet to think of his *Collected Works*
will come to you just before you enter
that neighborhood, you must pause
you must pause for long

# غيابهم

وماذا يظلّ
القليلُ
القليل
وقمصانهم،
قماشٌ على شجرٍ ينتشرُ.

وقمصانهم
رايةٌ لا تُشَدُّ
بغير الشَّجرْ.

ولا تُسْتَردُّ
ولكنها تنتصرُ.

## Their Absence

And what remains
but little little
and their shirts
fabric that spreads on trees
and their shirts

banners that tug
only at trees

and are not retrieved
a triumph

# أصابع

ما الذي يرنُّ في هُنيهَةِ السُّكوتْ
مُرهَفاً،
ما بين لَحْظَةِ الدَّمار
وانْتِفاضَةِ الحَريق.
أصابعٌ دَؤُوبَةٌ، حَكيمَةٌ
تُفكِّكُ المَدى بُيوتْ،
تَردُّهُ إلى مفاتِن
التُّراب والحَديدِ والبَشرْ
تُرتِّبُ السَّريرَ والثِّيابَ والصّورْ
حديقةً . . حديقةً
فيدخُلُ السَّلامُ في الحجرْ.

## Fingers

What's that ringing in the brevity of silence,
delicate between destruction's instant
and fire's eruption?
Unrelenting and wise
fingers disassemble the horizon
into houses and send it back
to the beauty of dirt, iron, and people

Fingers that make the bed,
fold clothes, and organize photos
one garden at a time
so that peace may enter stone

# دفاع

بيني وبينكَ يا فَتى
وطنٌ من الإسفَنج
تعصرهُ الحُروبُ العابراتُ
أمامَ منزلِنا
وينشُرهُ اَلأَملُ.


بيني وبينكَ أنّنا
نَختارُ مقصَلةً لنا
ونَطوفُ ﭺِ أَخشابِها .


ولدان من صُنع الكَلام
يُرَتِّبان المَوتَ وَالثَّمَرَ القَليلَ . .
ويَخجَلان
ويَخجَلان،
فَيَكذِبان
ويكذَبانَ
من الخَجَلِ.

## Defense

Between you and me, kid,
there's a homeland of sponge
that passing wars wring
in front of our house
where hope hangs it on a line

between you and me is that
we choose a guillotine for us
and we drift in its wood

two boys made of chatter
two boys arranging death
and a bit of fruit and are shy
so shy
they lie

**حراسة**

يبدأُ العازفونَ الرَّحيلَ البَطيءَ عن اللازمَةَ.

يَكسرونَ الكَلامَ
كآنية من زُجاج رَخيص
ويُلقونَ نحوَكَ باللائمَة.

ينتَهون.

سَنحفرُ وقتاً صَغيراً لنا في الحَجرْ
نُخَبِّئ أَلعابَ أطفالنا في يَديه
نُخَبِّئُ كلَّ الذي يَنكَسِرْ؛
تُرابَ الحَدائق
ماء الطَّريق
كلامَ الحَليفَ
جَدائل زوجَاتنا
صَمتهَُنَّ الجَليل،
وَنخرُجُ للمَوجَةَ الدّاهِمة.

## Night Watch

When the singers begin their slow departure
from refrains,
when they break talk like a bottle
of cheap glass and pitch
some blame our way,
when they're done with all that
     we'll dig
     a small time for us in rock
and hide our children's toys in its palms,
hide all fragile things
     the dirt of gardens
     water for the road
     the ally's word
     our wives' braids
     and their venerable silence
before we go out to meet the raiding wave

# اسُكونُ

هُناكَ لَوحَتانِ
وَمَقعدٌ طَويلٌ
وَوَردةٌ من القُماش
تَرتَخي على غُبارٍ.
هُناكَ وحشةٌ عَميقةٌ
تَلُفُّ نَفسَها
بِصَمتِ كائنينِ يَصمِتانِ.

. . الحَربُ ﰲ الحَديقةِ التي مَضَت
الحَربُ ﰲ غيابهم
الحربُ وَردَة على ثيابهم
الحَربُ بَيتُنا الجديدُ،
كلُبُنا الوَﰲِ
حَفلةُ الزَّواج
أُلفَةُ الخَرابِ.
الحَربُ مَلمَسُ التُّراب.

. . هَل نَحنُ كافيانِ وَحدَنا ؟
هَل تَكتَفي الدَّقائقُ التي تَعُدُّنا
بِرَقصة بَطيئة
وَخمرةٍ تَمُرُّ ﰲ ستائر المَكان !

*Stillness*


There are two paintings
and a long bench
and a cloth rose that has
slackened over dust,
there is coffee
and a stove alight
and a foreboding aloneness
that's wrapped itself
in the silence of two

In their absence there is war,
the rose woven into their clothes is war,
war is our new house
our loyal dog
our wedding party
the familiarity
of ruin
war
is loam in our finger webs

Are the two of us enough?
And the minutes that make promises to us
with a slow dance
and the liquor that passes through
the curtains of this place,
are they enough?

## الخَليل

لَيتَ أَنَّ المَدى
وَانْحِدارَ الزِّراعَة والخوخ واللوز وَالتّين
والصُّبيَةِ البالِغينَ.

لَيتَ أَنَّ القُرى
آه تلكَ القُرى . . ذاتَها
المُتعَبات من السَّيل والسَّير
والمَسجدُ المُنزَوي في الفَضاءِ الثَّقيلْ.

لَيتَ أَنَّ الأَغاني التي تَتركُ القَلبَ
خَيطاً من التَّبغِ أَو مَنزلاً خاسِراً في إِناء المَطَرْ.

لَيتَ أَنَّ النِّساءَ، الثِّيابَ، الكُهوف . .
التي خَبَّأَت عُريَ أَولادِنا في شِتاءِ الخَليلْ.

لَيتَ أَنَّ الخَليلْ
لم تَكُن بَلدةً في جَنوبِ الحَجَرْ.

*Hebron*

I wish that the horizon,
the farming terraces, almonds, peaches and figs,
and adolescent boys
I wish that the villages
oh, those same villages
that are wiped out
from walking and torrent
and that mosque that's tucked in a loaded space
I wish that the songs
that leave the heart as a tobacco thread
or leave a house defeated
in a pot for a leaking roof in the rain
I wish that the women
and clothes and caves
that hid our children's nakedness
in Hebron's winter
I wish that Hebron wasn't a town
in the south of stone

## أبو زهير

ويَمرُّ في الطُّرقات كي تنساهُ
في المقهى ليُذبلَ وَقتَهُ بالنَّرد
يدعو نَومهُ للنَّوم
يدعو ماءَهُ للشُّرب
ثمَّ يرشُّ زهراً في الحديقة للكَلام.
طفلٌ سَيترُكني ليلعبَ وحدَهُ،
هذا أبي
في آخرِ الأَيَّامْ.

*Abu Zuhair*


He passed through roads
so that roads would forget him
he passed time in a café
so that time would wither
in dice
and he called his sleep over for sleep
his water for a drink
then scattered some flowers
in the garden of speech

A child
who will leave me
to play by himself

that was my father
in his final days

## مساء ثالث

هل دقُّوا علَيك الباب
هل نادوك
أم مرّوا على أَطراف نيَّتِهم
وألقوا زهرةً لفنائكَ المُبتلّ ؟

هل حملوا اغاني الناس
فوق سروجهم ومضوا .

هل أعطوكَ رزقَ عيالِهم
ومَحبَّة الزَّوجات
والرّيفَ المنظَّم ﴾ ثِيابِ الأَهل .

كانوا خَمسةً وفَتى
وسابِعهُم سِراج اللَّيل .

# What do you think?

**OUR MISSION:**

*Poetry is vital to language and living. Copper Canyon Press publishes extraordinary poetry from around the world to engage the imaginations and intellects of readers.*

*Thank you for your thoughts!*

---

BOOK TITLE: _____

COMMENTS: _____
_____
_____

Can we quote you?  ☐ yes  ☐ no

☐ Please send me a catalog full of poems and email news on forthcoming titles, readings, and poetry events.

☐ Please send me information on becoming a patron of Copper Canyon Press.

NAME: _____

ADDRESS: _____

CITY: _____ STATE: _____ ZIP: _____

EMAIL: _____

 **Copper Canyon Press**
*A nonprofit publisher dedicated to poetry*

MAIL THIS CARD, SHARE YOUR COMMENTS ON FACEBOOK OR TWITTER, OR EMAIL POETRY@COPPERCANYONPRESS.ORG

CopperCanyonPress.org

## BUSINESS REPLY MAIL
FIRST-CLASS MAIL  PERMIT NO. 43  PORT TOWNSEND WA

POSTAGE WILL BE PAID BY ADDRESSEE

Copper Canyon Press
PO Box 271
Port Townsend, WA  98368-9931

*Third Evening*

Did they knock on the door while you were in?
Did they call your name or did they tiptoe
around their intentions
and throw some flowers for your wet patio?
Did they share their children's sustenance
and the love of wives
and the well-ordered countryside
in family outfits?
They were five and a boy
and their seventh a night's lantern

## مَعالِم

لم أَبِعْ جنَّتي
لم أُخِنْ صاحبي
لم أَكُنْ ذاتَ يوم
ثقيلاً على الأَصّدقاءِ.

كانَ بيني وبينَ المرافئِ
ماءٌ.

كانَ بيني وبينَ السُّهوبِ المُغطاة
بالثلج والليل
والزَّوَرقِ الآدَميِّ
التَّوحُّد ۓ موطن الذِّئب
والوحشة الأُمّ خَلْفَ العَواءِ.

كنتُ نصفَ المُكُوثِ ونصف السفر.

كنتُ بابَ المدينة ۓ سُورِها.
مرَّ بي الموتُ شائعة ۓ الطُرقِ
مرَّ بي الخوفُ أَرَضاً تلمُّ عن الأَرضِ
وشَمَ الأَثَرْ.
مرَّ بي البحرُ ۓ معطف الموج،
لا سمكَ البحر مُلكُ المياه
ولا الماءَ يملكُ أَن ينحسرْ.

كنتُ ۓ حلَّة الكائن المُستَريب انتباهاً لهُ
نابضاً ۓ مَسامَاتِه
تاركاً بابَ بيتي ومَدفأَتي
واثقاً
أَنَّ قلبي مَضى
دونَ أَن يعتَذِرْ.

*Landmarks*

I didn't sell my paradise,
didn't betray my companion,
never was a burden to friends,
there was always water
between me and ports,
there was always between me
and snow-covered prairies
a night and an Adamic boat,
the oneness of a wolf in his country
and a mother's dejection
after the howling

I was half travel, half residence,
I was the city gates on the city walls,
death passed me as a rumor on the road,
fear crossed my path as an earth that picks up
tattoo traces off the earth,
the sea passed through me
in a coat of waves,
neither fish is monarch over water
nor water possesses ebbing

I wore the attire of a suspicious being,
I was his attention

I pulsed through his pores
as I abandoned my house door,
my chimney,
confident that my heart had departed
without apology

ثلاثُ نوايا

١

سـأبكي لأنَدَمْ
وأترك قَلبي
على حجَرٍ مُوحشٍ في السُّهوبْ
وأركضُ في البَرِّ،
أركضُ في وَهمهم
في مَرايا الرَّصاص،
أهُشُّ الهَزيمةَ والنَّصرَ
والميّتين
بغُصنِ الحُروبْ.

٢

سَأرفعُ ظَهري كَذئْبٍ نبيلٍ
وأعوي على السُّهُبْ
حتى يُجَنّ
وحتى يَراني إلهُ الجُنود
قَتيلاً على وَعرِ الحربِ
أرضى وأَغضَبْ
وَبي وحشةٌ من بِحارٍ تَرنُّ
ثلاثينَ قَرناً
تَجيءُ وَتذهَبْ.

٣

أُنادي صَديقي
وأَترُكهُ واقفاً في الكلامْ.
أنادي حَبيبي
وأترُكهُ ساهِراً لا يَنامْ.

## Three Intentions

### 1

I will cry to regret
and slaughter my heart
on a desolate rock in the steppe
and run in the wilderness run
in their illusions in the mirrors
of bullets while shooing
victory and defeat
and also the dead
with war's twig

### 2

I will arch my back like a noble wolf
and howl in the plains
until the plains go mad
and the god of soldiers spots me lifeless
in war's meanness
I'd be pleased yet angry
and forlorn of seas that have tolled
for thirty centuries
they come and go

### 3

I call to my friend
and leave him standing in speech
I call to my lover
and leave her insomniac

موقع

بيـنَ التميمـة والدُّعاء،
أنا
أُفكِّرُ بالكلامِ
بنا
نحيفٌ، متعب..
أمضي إلى سَهري
كما يَمضي المحاربُ للكَمينِ،
وأختَفي سَنةً وراءَ ملابسي
ووظيفتي
فأرى العجائبَ كلَّها ...
وأنام.

*Position*


Between amulet and prayer
I think of speech,
of the two of us thin and fatigued,
and proceed
to my late night as a fighter
proceeds to his ambush

I disappear for a year
in my clothes in my job
see all sorts of wonders
then sleep

# منديل

لم يَعد بيننا ما يُقالُ
كُلُّ شيء مضى
في القطَار الذي خبَّأ الصّافرةَ،
في الدُّخان الذي لم يَصِر غَيمةً،
في الرَّحيلَ الذي لمَّ أطرافَكم.

لَم يَعُد بيننا ما يُقالُ،
فليَكن موتُكم
حكمةَ الفضَّة الباهرَةَ
ولتكُن شَمسُ تلكَ المُدُنْ
وَردةً فوقَ أكتافِكُمْ.

## Handkerchief

Nothing's left to say between us
everything went
into the train that hid its whistle
in the smoke that didn't become a cloud
in the departure that gathered your limbs

Nothing's left to say between us
so let your death be
the insight of dazzling silver
and let the sun of those cities
be a rose on your shoulders

# ظلال

نحن في فُسحة الباب
نَحرُثُ ظلَّ الظّهيرة والعَصر
نَزحفُ حتى غيابَ المَداخِنِ والظِّلّ.

وفي اللّيل
نَطرُقُ أحلامنا بالجدار.

نحنُ في فُسحة الباب،
نحرُثُ ظلَّ الظّهيرَةِ والعَصرُ.

وفي اللّيلِ
يُلقي بنا الياسَمينُ
بَعيداً عن البيت
حيثُ البنات الجَميلات يمضينَ للدَّيرِ.

وفي اللّيل
يخرُجُ نَعنَعنا من تُراب الحُقول
يُبَلّلُ وجهَ الهَواء الثّقيلَ
ويكسِرُ إبريقَهُ في الجوارِ.

نحنُ في فُسحة الباب
نرمشُ كي تَستَفيقَ الطّيور
لتَلقَطَ رُمّانَ أيّامنا
من إناءِ الغيابَ.

وفي اللّيل،
يَركضُ نَهرٌ إلى بيتنا
ولمّا ننامُ
يُدغدغُنا تَحتَ إبطِ القَميص
وَينفُخُ كي يَبردَ الشّاي.
وفي اللّيل
يحسبُنا «الآخرون» ظلالاً
فلا يَطرحونَ علينا السَّلام.

*Shadows*


We through the wide-open door
plow noon's and afternoon's shadows,
crawl until chimneys and silhouettes disappear
and at night
slam our dreams against the walls

We through the wide-open door
plow noon's and afternoon's shadows
and at night
jasmine thrusts us away from the house
where beautiful girls
head to the convent

And at night
out of the loam in the fields our mint
comes out to dampen the air's heavy face
and crack a nearby urn

We through the wide-open door
blink so the birds may wake up
and pick our days' pomegranates
from the jars of absence

And at night
a river runs to our house,
into our sleep, and through our shirts,
it tickles our armpits
and blows to cool our tea

And at night
the others think we are shadows
and don't say hello

from

# *The Heroism of Things*

1988

I'm mystified
how do I
rearrange the poem
everything's been said

# لو يَبكي الفَتى

أَشْعِلْ شُموعَكَ واكتَشِف قَلبي
وَلو يَبكي الفَتى
لَقَطَفْتُ زَهرة موتِه وأَكَلْتُها
وَرَقصتُ مَحنِيّاً عَلَى تَعبي
وَلرُبَّما نادَيتُ نومَتهُ إليَّ
وإذ أَمُدّ يَدي
لأَجْمَعَ ما تناثَرَ مِن أَغاني الأُمِّ عن كَتفيه
أَلمَسُ صَوتَها الدَّهريّ:
يا ذَهبي.

## If the Boy Could Cry

Light your candles, discover my heart
and if the boy could cry
I would pluck his death's flower
and eat it
then dance bent over my collapse

I might even call his slumber over to me
. . . and as I reach out my hand
to gather what has scattered
of his mother's songs over his shoulders
I touch her ageless voice:
        "My boy my gold"

مخدة

هل ظلَّ وَقتٌ كي أَقولَ لها :
مساءُ الخير يا أمّي
رَجعتُ بطلقة فـي القلب.
تلكَ مَخدَّتي
وَأُريدُ أن أرتاح.


قولي :
إنَّهُ يَرتاحُ
لَو دقَّتْ علينا الحَرب.

*Pillow*

Is there time left
for me to say to her
Good evening Mom
I'm back
with a bullet in my heart
and that's my pillow
I want to rest?

And Mom
if war knocks
say he's taking a rest

موتُ الفتى المدفعيّ

كلّما دَقَّت السّاعة العاشرة
سأُبصرهُ في جَحيم الضُّحى ذاك
يَركضُ والطائراتُ على كَتفه تَنحَني
ثُمَّ تَنقُرُ من صَدرهِ اللَّحمَ.

وهوَ أَطولُ منّي وأَصغَرُ عُمرا،
فَيَلتَفُّ كالقوس عشرَ سنين،
وَينزفُ أُخرى.

وَتبقى على كَتِفه الطائِرة.

## The Death of the Artillery Youth

Whenever the hour strikes ten
I see him
in the hell of noon . . . that one
running and the fighter jet stooping
over his shoulder
to peck the flesh off his chest

Taller and younger than I was
he would bend like a bow for ten years
and bleed another ten
and the jet
would remain
perched on his shoulder

تلكَ الحياة

ذاهبٌ كي أَرى كيفَ ماتُوا
ذاهبٌ نحوَ ذاكَ الخراب.

ذاهبٌ كي أَراهم هناك
هادئَينَ على تلّة الاشتباك.

كم الوَقتُ يا نرجسَ الأَربعاء
كَم الموتُ
كم كوكَب في يَد الأَرملة
خَمسةٌ او ثَلاثَة ؟
ثَوبُها كان يَزهُو
وكنّا
زُهوراً على ثَوبِها مُهملَة.

كم العُمرُ يا عتبات النِّساء
كم النَّهرُ
كم خنجرٍ في دَم الزَّوبعة
خَمسةٌ أو ثَلاثةَ ؟
تَركنا المَدينةَ تَلهُو
وَجئنا
لنُغلِقَ أَكفانَنا الذَّائعَة.

ذاهبٌ كي أَرَى كيفَ ماتُوا
ذاهبٌ نحوَ ذاكَ الخراب
ذاهبٌ كي أَرَى موتَهم
يا تلالَ الشَّمالِ  الشَّمال
يا هُبوبَ الجنوبَ الجنوب
ذاهبٌ كي أُنادي عَليهم بأسمائِهم :
انهَضُوا يا شَباب
انهَضُوا.

*That Life*

I'm going to see how they died
I'm going toward that wreckage
going to see them there
tranquil on the hill of engagement

Dear Wednesday's narcissus, what time is it
what death is it
what planet in the widow's hand
five or three?

Her dress was blooming
          we were
neglected flowers on her dress

Dear women's thresholds, how much is a lifetime
what time is a river
how many daggers in the blood
of the whirling storm
five or three?

We let the city play
and rolled our widespread shrouds shut

I'm going to see how they died
I'm going toward that wreckage
going to see their death
hills of the north
wind-rise of the south
I'm going to call them by their names

كانَ وَحدَه

لو تَهدأ العربياتُ
لو يَقف ارتجاج البابِ
لو يبكي الفَتى
لو تَرمش الكلماتُ بالمَعنى
ولو قُلنا له :
أمكُثْ هُنا .

لو لم يَعُد للبيت
لو أنّا طَرقنا مرَّةً أُخرى على الشُّبّاكِ
لو قالَت لنا الأبراجُ،
لو قالَت لَنا الأبراج.
لو كنّا هُناك
لو اتَّفقنا
لو أَفقنا لو أَفقنا .

كانَ يصرخُ كلَّما اهتَزَّ الزُّجاج.

## He Was Alone

If the cars would settle down
if the door would stop vibrating
if the boy would cry
if words had blinked
        their meaning
if we had told him
        Don't move stay here
if he hadn't left to go home
if we had knocked
once more on the window
if horoscopes and zodiacs had told us
if we were there
if we had agreed
if we had awakened
were awake

Whenever glass shook he would shriek

# حصار

سَنأتي على ذِكرِهم كلّهم
يومُنا حافلٌ والطّريقُ الطّريق
وَما زالَ يَأتي الأسى حينَ نَأسى.


أيُّنا سَوفَ يَنعسُ والليّلُ يَلمعُ كالسَّيف
أيُّنا سوفَ يَنسى!


كُلُّ أَرضٍ لَها أَهلُها
كُلُّ وقتٍ لهُ أهلُهُ
والزَّمانُ على نَحرِنا واقفٌ منذُ صيف.


لإيلاف إيلاف إيلافِهم
رَحلة البَرد والخَوف.


أَسكتُوا الطِّفلَ
لا تَتَرُكوا الأَرضَ تَبكي
ولا تَهِنوا
واحفَظُوا ظلَّهم
سوفَ نَذكُرهم كلّهم.


يومُنا حافلٌ، والطّريقُ الطّريق
وما زالَ يأتي الأسى حينَ نَأسى.


أيُّنا سوفَ يَنعَسُ والليّلُ يَلمعُ كالسَّيف
أيُّنا سوفَ يَنْسَى ؟

## Siege

We will remember all of them
in our crammed days, and the road is the road
and grief still comes when we grieve

Who of us will fall asleep when the night glistens
like a sword, who of us will forget?

Every land has its people
every time has its kin
and the place is theirs
and time for a summer now
has been standing
on our throats

I swear by what binds them by their harmony
and coalition

Silence that kid
don't let the land cry
don't be afraid
and remember their shadows
we'll remember them all

Our days are packed, the road is the road,
grief still comes when we grieve,
who of us will sleep,
night glistens like a sword,
who will forget?

# موتٌ جَماعيّ

لم يأتِ المَساءُ بغير عَتمَته
فَنِمْنَا لا سُقوفَ وَلَا عَراءَ.
وَلَم يَجئْ في اللَّيلِ ناجٍ
كي يُخبِرَنا بمَوتِ الآخَرين
وَظلّتِ الطُّرقاتُ تَصفِرُ
والمَكانُ يَعِجُّ بالقَتلى الذينَ أَتوا مِنَ الحَيِّ المُلاصِق.
كانَتِ الصَّرخاتُ تَفلِتُ نَحونا، فَنرى وَنسمَعُ
كيفَ يَمشي المَيّتُونَ على الهَواء
مُقَيَّدِينَ بخَيطِ دَهشَتِهِم، يَشُدُّ حَفيفَهُم أجسادَنا مِن قَشِّها
الوَضّاء.
نَصلٌ لامعٌ يَهوي عَلى الطُّرقات
« لم تَلِدِ النِّساءُ سوى الذينَ مَضُوا،
وَلَنْ تَلِدَ النِّساء. »

## Collective Death

Evening didn't come without its darkness
we slept roofless but with cover
and no survivor came in the night
to tell us of the death of others
        The roads kept whistling
and the place was packed with the murdered
who came from the neighboring quarter
whose screams escaped our way
        We saw and heard
the dead walk on air
tied by the thread of their shock
their rustle pulling our bodies
off our glowing straw mats
        a glistening blade
kept falling over the roads
        the women gave birth
only to those who passed
and the women will not give birth

هل سَيُصدِّقون

هَل يغفرُ الأولادُ للجيل الذي
دَكَّتْهُ خَيلُ الحربِ والمَنفى وَترتيبُ الذّهاب.


هَل سَيُفكِّرونَ بنا كَما كُنّا
كمائنَ في الشِّعاب
نَهُزُّ غيرَتَنا
وَننقُشُ في قَميص الأرض أشجاراً وَنجلسُ تَحتَها،
وَمُجازبينَ مُحاربينَ
نَهُشُّ غيمَ الحربِ من عَرباتها
وَنَجوسُ خلفَ حصارِنا الأَبَدِيّ
أو نَتَلقَّفُ القَتلى
كَفاكِهةٍ مُفاجئةٍ عَلى الأرضِ اليَبَابْ.


هَل يَغفرُ الأولادُ ما كُنّا
رُعاةَ الرّاجماتِ وَسادةَ المَنفى وَفَوضى الاحتلالِ
إذا أَشارَتْ نَحوَنا حَربٌ مُجاوِرَةٌ
نَهضْنا
كي نُرَتِّبَ في جَدائلها مَكاناً
صالحاً للحُبِّ والسُّكنى.


قليلاً ما استَراحَ القَصْفُ
قَليلاً ما رَأَينا الرّاجماتِ تَعودُ سالمة
قَليلاً ما قَطفْنا زهرةً لنُودِّعَ القَتلى وَنُكمل عُمرَنا.


لَو أَنَّ ذاكَ الصَّيفِ
أَعطانا قَليلاً من فَضاءِ الوَقتِ
قَبْلَ رَحيلِنا المَجنون!
هَل سَيُصدِّقون؟

## Will They Believe

Will the children forgive the generation
that's trampled by horses of war,
by exile and preparation for departure?

Will they think of us as we were,
a bunch of ambushes in ravines
we'd shake our jealousy
and carve trees into the earth's shirt
to sit under,
we, the factional fighters
who'd shoo the clouds of war out of their vehicles
and peer around our eternal siege
or catch the dead
like sudden fruit fallen on a wasteland?

Will the children forgive what we were,
some missile shepherds
and masters of exile and frenzied celebration,
whenever a neighboring war gestured to us
we rose
to set up in its braids a place
good for love and residence?

        The bombing rarely took a rest
the missile launchers rarely returned unharmed
we rarely picked flowers for the dead or went on
with our lives

If only that summer had given us a bit
of time's space before our mad departure

Will they believe?

## دير أريحا

لم تأت لنا آلهة منه
وكانَ يَشِي بهبوطِ الله.

خطواتُ الرهبانِ المرسومة كالآيات
حفيفُ ملابسهمَ ينشقُّ خفيفاً في اَلرّدهاتِ
الهمس
وكفُّ الرّاهب بيضاء كالشمعِ
على شعري المقصوصِ
وضحكته البيضاء.

كأنَّ اللهَ سيهبطُ من شفتيه
الآن.

## Jericho's Convent

No gods ever came to us from there,
though it used to suggest God's descent

The priests' footsteps were drawn like verses
and in the corridors
the rustle of their robes would rip a bit

The whispers and the priest's hand candle-white
on my freshly cut hair
and his laugh white

As if God were about to descend
from his lips

مرآة

كأسرى في حُرُوب لم يخضها الجيش
رتلاً يهبطون إلى المزارع
يحفرُون ويحفرُون
ويطلقون هناك أحواضاً وأقنية
وأقنية وأحواضاً ولا يتوقفون.

*Mirror*


Like prisoners of some war an army didn't fight
they descend in file to the farms
they dig and dig and liberate
basins and canals
basins and canals and never stop

مـرآة

وجهان في البلوى
أبي وحِصَانهُ
قمرٌ صغير قربَ منزلنا الصغير.
سنصيدهُ.
لو أرجعونا للطفولة، مرّة أُخرى،
سنحبسه قليلاً، قبل أن ينشقَّ قلبانا
فنتركه
يطير.

*Mirror*

Two faces in catastrophe:
my father and his horse

A small moon near our house,
we'll hunt it

If only they'd return us to childhood once more
we'd detain it for a while
until our two hearts split

then we'd let it fly

علاقة

بدّلتُ نصفَ دفاتري وجلستُ قربك
أُرمي يدي لتراك،
أرجعها وألمس ما رأتْ
وأقولُ في سرّي أنا:
أرضى بما يُرضاهُ قلبك.


سنعوم في المجرى معاً
سننامُ قربَ النهر كالإسفنج تخرج من ثنايانا المياه
سنختفي في الصمت
نُنصتُ هادئين ونرتخي فنرى تنفّسنا
ونسمعُ كيفَ ينمُو العُشب تحت مظلّة الشجر القصير
وكيفَ تنحدر الفراشات الجديدة من ضلوع الظل
كيفَ تفتشُ الألوان عن أشكالها الأولى
فتسقط زهرةً في حقل
أو خيطاً على منديل.


ندخل نومة الأشياء
نتركُ خلفنا المرآة مُشرَعة كبيتِ الجنّ
نتركُ خلفنا الصبيان والحارات،
والشمس التي سقطت كقُبّعة عن الأشجار،
فانكشفت لنومتنا قرون «البنسيان» المُرّ.


ننسَى أنهم بعثُوا صغيراً «للخرابة»
حيث يندفن الصغار.

## Relationship

I exchanged half my books to sit near you
and released my hands
so they could see you
then retrieved them to touch what they saw

I said to myself
what satisfies your heart is good for mine

Together we floated in the current
slept like sponges by the river
soaked up the water that seeped from its folds
as we disappeared in silence
relaxed and loosed to watch
our breaths and listen to grass grow
under a canopy of shrubs
how butterflies slope down from the ribs of shadow
how colors search for their primary shapes
a flower fallen on ground
a thread in a handkerchief,
we entered the sleep of things
left behind the mirror pitched like a house of jinn
left behind girls and boys, alleyways and the sun
that fell like a hat off trees
and exposed us to the bitter branches
of holm oak

We forget that they sent a boy to the junkyard
where children are buried

موتٌ آخر

جثَّتها أَمامَ الباب
وقفتها هُناك، غناؤها يِّ اللَّيل، لَمعةُ مشطها الفضِّيّ
رُكبتها التي تَرمي لنا برقاً
خواتمها الزّجاج،
وشعرها المغسول بالحنّاء، هزَّة رأسها الوثنيّ،
ضحكتها أَمامَ الباب،
مَعنى أَن تَردَّ الشَّعرَ أَو ترخيه
حين تمرُّ يِّ ألق من « الزّاروب » دّراجاتنا وتصيح
أجراس وأبواق فيرقُص قلبها وَيرفّ.

ثَمة طوبتان تُحاصران الرَّأس
ثُمَّ ذراعها المَمْدُود عَبر الباب
خمسُ أَصابع يِّ الكفِّ، بعضُ مناجلٍ يِّ الرّيح
زينتها أَمامَ الباب
غُرَّتها  ودهشتها،
ودهشَتنا أَمام قَميصها المفتوح.

صَباح الخير
وجهُك بارد وَيداك باردتان.
صباحُ الخير
وحدَك تذهبَين الآن
وحدَك تخرُجين إلى الطَّريق بلا خواتمك الزُّجاج
بلا التّماعة رُكبتيك
ستهدرُ الأَصواتُ حولك والرِّجال سيهدرون
ويهدرُ السَّيلُ المخبأ يِّ الصُّخور
ستزعقُ العرباتُ يِّ السّوق الكبير
ويركضُ الأَولادُ مزهوّين يِّ المرآة.

وحدَك تخرُجين  إلى الطَّريق
تُبلِّلين الأَرض والملَح العنيد
وتخجَلين من المرور أَمامنا
سيطيرُ ثَوبك يا فتاة.

*Another Death*


Her corpse is in front of the door
her standing there, singing at night, the glare of her silver comb
her knee that darts lightning our way
her glass rings

her henna-washed hair and pagan headshake
her laugh by the door
her gist in throwing her hair back or letting it down

. . . Then through the narrow alley
our lightning bikes would pass
and bells and horns would sound and her heart
would dance and flutter

. . . Two bricks besiege her head,
one arm is stretched through the door,
five fingers in hand, some sickles in the wind,
her jewelry by the doorstep
her forehead and shock
and our surprise at her opened shirt

Good morning . . .
your face is cold, your hands are cold
Good morning . . .
alone you now go

Alone you now go out to the road without your glass rings
or radiant knees, the voices around you
will squall, men will bawl, the flood hiding in stone
will roar, carriages in the grand market will shout
and the kids will run vainglorious in mirrors

Alone you go out to the road
to wet the ground and obstinate salt,

وستهدُر « السَّلط » البعيدة ﰲ الجبال
سيهدُر « العدوان » فوق خيولهم
وسيعبرون النَّهر، من أقصى « الخاضة »
حيثُ تتحسرُ المياه.


وأنت وحدَك تخرُجين بلا مفاتيح الغرف
وبلا وصايا الأُمّ
تتكشف الطريق أمام خطوَك، ثمَّ وحدك
فجأةً سُتباغتين النَّهر يلمعُ وحده
خيطاً من البلّور علَّقهُ إله.


وستُبصرين « الدير »
فانوساً تدلله « أريحا » حين ينعسُ زيتهُ
وتهزُّ تحت نُعاسه قلقُ الصَّلاة.


وستُبصرين « السَّيلَ »
والبدو الذين تّخلَّعوا، كخزانة سَقطتْ مفاصلُها
وظلَّ الماءُ يهدُر حولَهم حتى أنتهوا للنَّهر
موتٌ ظلَّ يركضُ بيننا،
ويهزُّ نومتنا ، فننهضُ كي نراه.


وأنت ترتحلين
ينعسُ ﰲ يديك الضَّوء
ينعسُ ﰲ يديك النَّهر
ينعسُ ﰲ يديكَ السَّيل
ينعسُ ﰲ يديكَ الصَّخر
تبرقُ بقعةٌ ﰲ « الحوش »
كنت هناك تغتسلين.


وحدَك تخرُجين إلى الطَّريق
تُبلِّلين الأرضَ والملحَ العنيد، وَتخجَلين،ا
وَتخجَلين.
تهُبُّ رائحةٌ من الأُخدود،
يزعقُ لقلقٌ ﰲ الجوِّ،
يرمقُنا غُرابُ الموت، يندَهُنا عن الطُّرقات أطفالاً
فَنتبعهُ بأَرجلنا الصَّغيرة، صائحين، مُهلِّلين.

too shy to pass in front of us . . .
your dress will fly, girl

And the town far in the mountains will bellow,
the enemies on horseback will howl,
the enemy brothers!

Did they hear the news and come?
Twice they'll cross the river, from the far corner
where water recedes

And alone you go out, without room keys
or mother's counsel

The road clears up before your steps then suddenly alone
you surprise the river . . . radiant . . . a crystal thread
hung by a god

You'll spot the convent, a lantern
that Jericho pampers:
whenever its oil falls asleep
Jericho rocks the angst of prayer

And you'll witness the flood,
and the Bedouins who come apart like a closet
with unhinged doors
next to the water that keeps roaring around them
and guides them to the river

A death kept running between us, shook our sleep
so we would rise to see it

And as you depart
light falls asleep in your hands
the river falls asleep in your hands
the flood falls asleep in your hands
stone falls asleep in your hands

and a spot in your courtyard flashes
where you used to bathe

Alone you go out to the road
to wet the ground and obstinate salt, turn shy, too shy

A gully emits a smell
a stork honks in air
the crow of death throws us a stare, calls us in
from the roads . . . children
we follow him with our small feet
screaming and cheering

خليل زقطان

وسأنحني لأَشمَّ رغبتَهُ،
زهورَ مقامه ورخامه
وذبول بهجته ...
وتبديلَ الغواية بالرضى.
وأردُّ عنهُ البردَ والزوّارَ والدّفلى
وأولادَ الحرامْ.
وأقول:
أكثر من سيُشبهني أبي ...
عثراتهُ البيضاء والوهم الذي قَطَفَ الكلام.


صيحةٌ تمشي على قدمين واهنتين
ترمقني بصيف عذابها ...
وترشّني بالماء كي أخضرَّ.
تنفضُ عن أظافرها التراب المرِّ.
... ذاك أبي
بكى من عتمةٍ في القبر!


وألمُّ بيتَ غيابكَ المُلقى..
كأنّا وحدنا في الأرضِ
أنتَ تموت
كي أطوي جناحَ النسر بعدَ رحيلهِ
وأصدّق الصمتَ الذي يبقى.

*Khalil Zaqtan*

And I will bend down to smell his desire
his tomb's flowers and marble
his wilting joy
his swapping temptation for content

And I will keep him from the cold, visitors, oleander,
and the sons of bitches and say: No one
will resemble me like my father
his white stumbling and the illusion that plucks words

A shout that walks on two feeble legs
eyes me with the summer of discontent
and sprinkles me with water, turns me green
before it shakes the bitter dirt
off its fingers
. . . that's my father
he cried from a darkness in the grave

And I will gather the house of your chucked absence
as if we were alone on Earth
. . . you die
so I can fold the falcon's wings after its departure
and believe the silence that remains

تمهّلي يا بنت

قلْ للبحيرة أنْ تنام
وقلْ لصاحبة القميصِ اللّيلَكيّ:
تمهّلي لنراكَ أكثرْ.

لن نُحبّك يا فتاةُ، ولن نُطيلَ العمر، لن نتصيّدَ الأوهامَ
لن نبكيَ على عسل الكلام، ذهابنا نادى
وثمّة مركبٌ هَتَفَتْ وأسلحةٌ وخوذاتٌ وعسكرْ.

قلْ للمدينة أن تردَّ على أخي طرفَ الغطاءِ
وأنْ تُهَدْهدَ قَلْبَهُ حتى أجيءَ، إذا رجعتُ،
لكي أعلّقُ في يديه البحرَ والمدنَ البعيدةَ
والقرى الملقاة في طُرق الجنودِ
وهَمْهَمَات الرّيح في مَطَرات مَنْ ماتوا
وأوهامَ القصيدةِ، والشراعَ الحر، والموت المبكّر.

قُلْ للحياة تمهّلي في السير
لم تتهيّأ المرآةُ
لم تتزيّن الفتياتُ، لم يَرقُصنَ، لم يرمينَ منديلاً
ولم يعجنّ سكّر.

قُلْ للحياة تمهّلي في السير
إنَّ بناتنا ما زلْنَ في المَتراسَ
وانتظري قليلاً، لحظةً أخرى،
فثمة جيلُنا المحنيُّ تحتَ النار.
طوبى للرجال وهمْ يرشُّون القَصيدةَ بالمياه
ويتركونَ القلبَ فانوساً على أفقٍ تكسّر.

قُلْ للحياة
تمهّلي يا بنتُ واقتربي
لنلمسَ صدرَك الملكيَ بالكفّين
كي يخضرَّ مذهولاً ومرويّاً وحيراناً
كإقليمٍ مِنَ الزعترْ.

## Slow Down, Girl

Tell the lake to sleep,
tell the woman with the lilac shirt to wait up
so we can see more of her

Girl, we won't love you, won't extend our life, won't hunt delusions
or cry over the honey of words,
our departure has called, some boat
has blown its horn, some weapons, helmets, and soldiers

Tell Russeifa to tuck my brother in
and dandle his heart until I return, if I return

to hang on his hands the sea, the distant cities
and scattered villages in the soldiers' paths,
the wind that mutters rain showers of the deceased,
the poem's illusion, the free sail, and premature death

Tell life: Slow down,
a woman is not ready yet,
some girls haven't tried their makeup on or danced
or tossed their hankies or kneaded sugar wax

Tell life: Slow down,
our girls are still at the barricades,
we haven't written our names on trees or run
except from shelling

Wait up a bit, another moment, here
is our generation huddled under fire:
blessed be the ones who sprinkle the poem with water
and leave the heart as a lantern for a fractured horizon

Girl, tell life to slow down
and come close, girl, so we can touch your bare chest

with our palms,
turn it green, astonished and quenched
like a province of thyme

غيابهم

يرفُّ ثم يثقلُ الهواء
يحطُّ غامضاً على يدي وينحني
لينقرَ الكلامَ من مسائي البطيء.


زجاجةُ النبيذ
كلما ناديتهم
تُضيء.

## Their Absence

flutters before the air turns heavy
then alights mysterious on my hand . . . and bends
to peck the speech of my sluggish evening
the wine bottle
whenever I call out to them
lights up

## أشيائي تلك

وأُريدُ كي أَغفو
يدا من فضة بيضاءَ،
قلباً جلَّلته المُغفرة.
وأُريدُ كي أَغفو
نبيذاً ساحراً، كنبيذ ذاكَ الليل،
حين غَلَبَتْني يا رقصُ، وارتَجَفَتْ على كتفيَّ أُغنيةٌ
وطارتْ قبّرة.
وأُريدُ من ذَهَبَتْ، كما ذَهَبَتْ
مبلَّلة بماء القلب.
وأُريدُ كي أَغفو رسائلَ من أُحب
وصورتي طفلاً تكلِّل نومتي أُمّي
وحولي العائلة.

وأُريدُ كي أَغفو كلامَ أبي وزينة روحِه
ورنينَ بهجته صباحَ العرس،
آنيةَ نحاسٍ والنساءُ مجلَّلاتٍ يرتجفنَ على هزيم الرقصِ
والأقدام والدنيا غبارُ.
عشرونَ رمحاً إخوتي
أكتافهمْ لَعِبَتْ هناكَ ترنَّحت
غبنا وعُدنا
وهي تصعدُ في الهواء وترتخي،
كأسٌ على أكتافهم قلبي يطوفُ
ولا يُدارُ.

وأُريدُ عزفاً ساحراً، جذلاً، وموسيقى،
وموسيقى قديمة.
وأُريدُ أَنْ يدنو منَ الشبّاك دوريٌّ
وأَنْ يأتي إليَّ السَنديان.
وأُريدُ أَنْ أبكي بكاءً جارحاً.
وأُريدُ أَنْ تتهيّأوا للانصرافِ جميعكم.
وأُريدُ أَنْ لا تذهبي.

## My Things

To fall asleep
I need a hand of white silver
and a heart cordoned with pardon

To fall asleep I need magic wine
like the wine of that night when dancing conquered me
and a song trembled on my shoulder
and a lark flew

And I need the one who left just as she left
wet by the heart's water

To fall asleep I need the letters my love wrote
and that photo when I was asleep as a kid
while my mother laureled my sleep
and the rest of the family surrounded me

And I need my father's words, his soul's ornament,
I need his joy's ring on the morning of wedding

And a copper pot and beloved women who shake
from the rumble of rhythm their feet and a world of dust

I need a virtuoso and I need music and glee,
especially old music

And I need a house sparrow
to come to the window
and holm oak to come to me

And I need my crying to wound me
and for all of you to get ready
to leave

All of you,
and God, and the devil, and the prophet man

And I need you to stay

غيرة

أَمشي وأَهبطُ وردتين
وأَنحني لرنينِ ضحكتها
وأَهبطُ وردةٍ أُخرى
فأَلمسُ جنّة الحنّاء.
مخمورٌ وبي جذلٌ
وأَرقصُ ملءَ أُغنيتي.
أنا العربيّ
أَحلمُ أَنْ أُحبّك في المساء
لكي تلمّي في الصباحِ عن الحديقة
غِيرَتي السوداء.

## Jealousy

I walk, climb down as two roses,
and bend to the ring in her laugh
then again descend as another rose
      to touch her henna's paradise,
intoxicated and cheerful
      I dance to my song's fill
I the Arab
who dreams that I love you in the evening
so that by morning you'd gather
away from the garden
my jealousy black

جَدَل

في موقف الباص القريب وَقَفْنَ
طالبتان وامرأةٌ وريح.

يا ريحُ قبّعتي من القشّ الفصيح
ومعطفي رثٌ ومنديلي مطر.
جذلُ القصائد في خطاي
وفي يدي دنيا مدلّلة
صنعتُ هواءَها
وسماءَها
وحنينَ فتْيَتها ونرجسَ ثوبها.
وجمعتُ ذاكرةً لأكتُبها
وأصحاباً أرشّ بهم براري الملح كي تخضرَّ.
واستغربتُ من نفسي، أنا المغتَرّ،
من كفّيّ حين ألُمّ أحجاراً وأثماراً
وناساً من جحيم الأرض
ثم أعيدهم شعراً يكادُ الحلمُ يطفرُ منه.

واستغربتُ من نفسي، من الأشياء
وهي بسيطةٌ كالماء.

قبّلَني الإلهُ على فمي فأضاء.
أطلقَني على اسمي، وناداني به
فنزلتُ من جسدي لأنظرَ حولهُ
فرأيتُ
واستغربت.

زرتُ قصيدتي في بيتها
ودفنتُ زينتها الغبية في الترابِ
وقلتُ للكلمات
لا تأتينَني صفّاً على طبق الخلاص،
مجلّلاتٍ بالترقّبِ والنحيبِ، مهيّآتٍ للخلاص.

مُحاورات عاصيات جئنَ لي
كيما أشدُّ «الزورقَ السكران» من كمّ التأمّل

## Glee

They stood at the bus stop,
two schoolgirls, a woman, and a wind:
Wind, my hat is made of literary straw,
my coat is tattered, my hankie a rain

The glee in poems trails my steps
and in my hand there's a pampered world
     whose air
     sky
     and the tenderness
     of its youth
     the narcissus of its garment
     I made

To write a memory I gathered a memory
and to green the marshes I sprinkled friends
over the salt marshes and was at a loss
with myself, I the conceited, at a loss
with my palm as I collected stones,
fruits, and people from the hell of the earth
to return them as poems
that dreams almost leap out of

I was at a loss with myself and with things
as simple as water

A god had kissed me on the mouth and lit up,
he had released me to my name then called me by it,
I stepped down from my body
to look about him and saw and was
at a loss

I visited my poem in its house,
buried its dumb ornament in the dirt

كِي يراني بينما أَمشي، أنا المغتَرُّ،
أحلمُ أَن أَعيدَ النورَ للعميانِ
والتفكير للحمقى

ولستُ سوى الذي يمشي على قدميهِ جَذْلاناً
أمام الباص.

and told words:

> Don't come to me
> a line on salvation's platter, exalted
> in anticipation and wailing, primed
> for deliverance!

Interlocutors and disobedient they came:
whichever way I tugged at the drunken boat
in my contemplation's depths, that it might
see me as I walked, I the conceited,
dreaming of giving light
back to the blind, thought
back to the foolish
when I'm only one

who's merrily walking
in front of the bus

## لو نِمْتَ قُربي أَمس

لو نَمْتَ قربي أمس
لو ناديتني
لو مِلْتَ وامتدّت يداك إلى حريرِ الرّوحِ
لو أَيْقظتني من نومة العميان
كُنتَ عرفتني وغلبتني
ولَمَسْتَ خيطَ البرقِ في جسدي.
بعشرِ أصابعٍ تتكلّمُ العينان.


لو ناديتني
لابتلَّ ريشٌ مسائنا، ولقادَنا عسلٌ
إلى غرفٍ من الطينِ المجفّف تحتَ عينِ الشمس
فوقَ ترابها المرشوشِ بالماء المهيّأ للوضوء
هتفتُ بالجسد :
اكتشفْ بلواك!
ثم حملتهُ لأظلّ فيه.
لمستهُ بيديكَ فابتهجتْ به روحي
سمعتُ حنينهُ في النوم فاستغربتُ
ثم رأيتُ نرجسةً تضيءُ هواءَهُ
فمشيتُ
أطوي وردةَ الدنيا وأتركُ ثيةً
لأراك.
مأخوذاً أجفّفُ رغبتي بالعشبِ.
مقهوراً ومحبوباً ومكشوفاً
وبي ألقُ الهلاك.

## Had You Slept beside Me

Had you slept beside me last night
had you called to me
had you leaned and stretched your arm to my soul's silk
had you woken me up from the sleep of the blind
   you'd have known me and overcome me,
touched the lightning thread in my body:
a pair of eyes speaks with ten fingers

Had you called to me
our evening's feathers
would've gotten wet, some honey
would've led us to rooms of dry mud
where over its water-sprinkled dirt
and ablution water I would have shouted
at my body:
   Figure out your affliction
Lord!
Then I would have carried my body to remain
within it, would have touched it with your hands
to delight my soul, heard its longing
in sleep and marveled at it
as I saw narcissus illuminate its air, the air
in which I'd walk, fold
life's rose except for one petal
so I could see you

Baffled,
I dry my desire with grass,
   oppressed, beloved, exposed
and full of perishing radiance

# نَحْنُ هُنَاك

أَقولُ وقدْ أَخَذَتْ كلَّ شيءٍ:
سيبقى الذي لا يراهُ سِواي
بريقُ الكلامِ ولونُ الستائرِ
لمّا تشيرُ إلىَ زورقٍ في الظلام.
ترّدُها في الفراشِ
ورائحةُ البنّ في قَلبها واحتراقُ البخّور.

سيبقى الذي لا يراهُ سِواي
البكاء المعدّ على عجلٍ للسحور
النعاسُ المبلَّل،
والخوفُ من أنّنا وحدنا بعد عام.

أَقولُ وقد أَخَذَتْ كلَّ شيءٍ
وشدَّتْ على خصرها معطفاً من نجومٍ سعيدة
وأيضاً، معاً، وحدنا في القصيدة.

*We Are There*


This is what I say now that she's taken everything

The things that only I see will stay behind:
the glimmer in our talk and the color of curtains
when she points to a boat in the dark

her hesitancy in bed
the smell of coffee in her heart and the burning incense

Only the things I see will stay behind:
the crying prepared in a hurry before fasting begins,
the damp sleepiness
        and the fear that after a year we'd be alone

This is what I say now that she's taken everything
        and wrapped around her waist a sweater
with happy stars . . .
        and also that we're together, alone, in the poem

سيرة

أَتيتُ لأَكتفي بالودِّ،
لن أبقى
فبي عبثٌ، وبي فوضى
وبي دُنيا ودِين.

وبين أن أرضى وأشقى
نومة الغفران في أرضٍ من الحمقى
وصحبةٍ كافرين.

ولم يزلْ قلبي يضيءُ
وسوف تطرقهُ النساءُ، كما تعوّدتْ النساءُ
ليسترحن من الرجالِ الآخرين.

## Biography

I came and was satisfied with affection
I won't stay
there's absurdity in me there's chaos
there's life and religion
and between contentment and affliction
there's what I want and what I don't want
and between coming and leaving
there's the sleep of redemption
in a land of fools
and the company of infidels

My heart still lights
and women will keep knocking on it
as some women do to take a rest
from other men

## فَرحٌ بأشيائي

فَرحٌ لأنَّ يدي معي
فَرحٌ ومبتهجٌ لأنَّ يدي معي
تهتَزُّ حولي، ثم أرفعها سعيداً كي أُلوِّحَ للفتاة.
أَرُدّها وأقول:
ها .. حُريّتي جنبي
وها .. قلبي
وها كَتِفي الذي لَمَعتْ على أبنوسِه
قَبلُ الحياة.

فَرح بأنَّ الريحَ بلَّلتِ المساءَ فبلَّلتْ كفّي
وهزَّتْ مضجعي.
فَرحٌ ومبتهجٌ بأنَّ يدي التي نادَتك
أو لَمَسَتك
أو ضَمَّتَك
ما زالت مَعي.

فَرحٌ بصوتي، نبرةُ الريف الثقيلة في ملامحه
وفيه سعادةٌ حمقاءُ تعجبني.
ويصلحُ للقراءة والغواية والغناء ـ إذا شربتُ ـ
وللمودّة حين أَفتقدُ الدليلَ، وللتلاوة والتأمّل،
فهو يصلحُ للتأمل حين يهجرُ بيتهُ العالي
ويجمعُ نرجساً للبنت.

فَرحٌ بصوتي، حين أنَّهُ صاحبي الماشي بلا سببٍ
على زهرِ الحديقةِ ذابلاً كالموت.

فَرحٌ ومُبتهجٌ بصوتي، وهو يُشبهني
ويهدأ حينما أشتاقُ أو أبكي
ويدخلُ في ملابسه الثقيلة إذْ أضمّك.
ثم يخرجُ حافياً في الليل مَنّي
كي يُرتّبُ نفسهُ لحروفَ نومك.

فَرحٌ بأشيائي وقلبي.
فَرِحٌ بكل حقائقي.

## Happy with My Things

### 1

Happy because I have my hand,
happy and thrilled because my hand's with me
shaking about me until I raise it and wave to a woman

I put it down and say:
Here, my freedom's by my side,
here's my heart
and my shoulders whose ebony
is radiant with life's kisses

Happy that the wind soaked the evening and wet my palm
and shook my bed,
happy and thrilled that my hand, which called to you
or touched you
or hugged you,
is still with me

### 2

Happy with my voice . . . its distinct country tone
and its foolish joy that I like,
good for reading, singing, and seduction when I drink,
good for company when I lack a guide,
good for recitation, for reflection, especially
reflection when my voice abandons
its home in the heights and gathers
some daffodils for a woman

I'm happy with my voice . . . when I call to my friend
who aimlessly walks on garden flowers
that are wilted like death

بالأصدقاء على تردّدهم وقلّتهم،
بملمس وجَنتيكِ وصوتكِ الغالي
وسحرَ خطيئتي ورنين صدري
فَرحٌ بِما صَنَعَتْ بيَ الدنيا، وما صَنَعَتْ يداي بها
ومُبتهجٌ بعمري.

Happy and thrilled with my voice as it resembles me,
as it calms down when I'm crying or in longing,
as it puts on its old clothes . . . as I hug you,
as it walks out of me barefoot in the night
to arrange itself for the alphabet
of your sleep

   3
Happy with my things . . . and my heart,
happy with all my truths,
with my friends who are few and frequent,
with the touch of your cheeks and your cherished voice,
with my sin's magic and my echo's ring,
with what life made of me
and what my hands made of it
and thrilled with my life

أَساوِرك المَاكرات

الرقصُ سيّدتي
منازِلنا الصغيرة حول قلبك،
غرفةُ الريح الأثيرة،
آخرُ البرق المعلّق نرجساً، بريّةً
لدفوفِ ثوبك.

والرقصُ سيدتي
شعاعُ الروح
آنية الغرام الحرِّ
نافذةُ الجَروح
معابدٌ بيضاء
أقواسٌ
وأنثى ﻓﻲ ثيابِ الطير.

الرقصُ
ذاكرةُ السلالة
نجمةُ الأجدادَ إذْ يمضُون
أبراجٌ
وصيّادون.

والرقصُ سيّدتي
هتافُ الأرض ﻓﻲ أجسادنا.
شيخُ الحروبَ وأوّلُ الصلوات.
فرحةُ أنْ أراكِ ترتبين سرير نومتِنا
عذوبةُ أنْ أدقَّ على جدار الشَّقّة الأخرى
ليأسرني الجواب.
نسيجُ دهشتِنا، انفتاحُ الباب.

جيشٌ غامضٌ يأتي بموسيقاه عبرَ النافذة
ودخولنا ﻓﻲ اللوزِ كي نأتي بتوتِ الأغنيات.

الرقصُ سيّدتي
رحيلك ﻓﻲ الصباح بلا حقيبتك الخرز
وبلا أَساورِك الثلاَث المَاكرات.

## Your Cunning Bracelets

Dancing, my dear,
is our small houses around your heart,
the wind's favorite room,
the tail end of lightning as it hangs on
to narcissus in a prairie for the tambourines
of your dress

Dancing, my dear,
is the soul's radiance, the urn of free passion,
the window of wounds and white shrines,
arches and a woman
in a bird's outfit

Dancing is a memory of a lineage,
the star of forebears,
horoscopes, and hunters,
the earth chanting in our bodies,
the old man of war, the first prayer,
and the joy of my seeing you prepare
our bed for the night

It's the charm that makes me knock on the wall
of the neighboring apartment
to imprison myself
in the reply

It's the fabric of our surprise,
a door opening, a mysterious army that arrives
with its music through the casement,
and our entrance into almond trees to get
to the berries of songs

Dancing, my dear,
is your departure in the morning

without your beaded purse
or your three
cunning bracelets

أَبْعَدُ مِنْ ذَلِك

إنَّ بي رغبة أن أرى الأرض.
أنْ أستعيدَ التلاوة من حكمةِ المُقرئين.
أنْ أفكّرَ كالنسر.
إنَّ بي رغبة أن أرى الأرضَ كاملةً.
أنْ أُعيدَ الغناءَ إلى الشعر.
أنْ أنادي الجبال الغريبة:
يا ... إخوتي.
وأنْ أُفلتَ القلبَ من جثّة الشوق
من عسَلِ الأنبياءِ الثقيلَ.

ربما لم يزلْ في أعالي الجبال
ليلكٌ غيرَ عينيك
أو فضّةٌ غير صوتك.

ربما لم تزلْ
في مكان بهيٍّ ومغتسلٍ بالخطايا
صيحةٌ لَم تُقلْ
معدنٌ لم يُجَسّ
رغبةٌ لم تصلْ.

يا حبيبي الذي لن أُسمّيه إلاَّ حبيبي
في يدي زهرةُ العمرِ توشكُ أنْ تحترقْ
فأرجوكَ
أرجوكَ
أنْ نفترقْ.

## Beyond That

I have a wish to see the land,
a wish to retrieve recitation from the wisdom of lectors
and to think like a falcon

I have a wish to see the land whole,
return song to poetry,
call strange mountains my brothers
and release my heart from the corpse of longing
and from the thick honey of prophets

Perhaps there still remains in mountaintops
a night besides your eyes
a silver besides your voice
perhaps there still remains
in some beautiful place washed down with sin
a scream to be shouted
a metal to be examined
a desire unattained

My love, whose name is just that, "my love,"
my life's flower
is about to burn in my hand
I beg you
please
         let's part

### أجساد على العشب

على مهلٍ خبَّأَتنا النساءُ
على مهلٍ صُغْنَ من فضّة الأغنيات
دروعاً لأيّامنا الهائجة.
على مهلٍ ألقت الشمسُ رمّانةَ الضوءِ
نحو السهّول.
على مهلٍ أرسَلَ القَلبُ أغصانهُ في الحقول.
على مهلٍ أطلقتنا الجرارُ
وأنضجتِ الخبزَ أفرانُنا.
على مهلٍ أيقظتنا الحروب ودارت بنا عربات السباق.
على مهلٍ جاء مهرُ الفراق
بهيّاً على زرقةٍ هانئة.
على مهلٍ ...
نارنا هادئة.

*Bodies on Grass*


Patiently the women hid us
patiently they forged out of the silver of songs
shields for our agitated days
patiently the sun flicked the light's pomegranate
toward the plains
patiently the heart sent its branches to the fields
the jars released us
the ovens baked our bread
patiently wars woke us and race cars took us
for a spin
patiently departure's colt came
beautiful on a blessed blue
patiently our fire
is slow

## جميعهم

تتعبُ البنتُ التي خلفَ الإطار.
تتعبُ البنتُ التي تكنُسُ حوشَ البيت
من فوضى الزواج.
تتعبُ البنتُ التي في القلب.
تتعبُ البنتُ التي قبّلتُها في عتمةِ الدوّار
من عشر سنين.
تتعبُ البنتُ التي غنّتْ على مفرقِ «ناعور»:
افترقنا، فابتهج .. يا ذئب.
تتعبُ البنتُ التي أهديتها شعراً
ولم تفهمه.


يتعبُ الشعرُ الذي يأتي من الأريافِ مشياً
يتعبُ العائدُ من أوهامه حيّاً
وفي عينيه أجراسٌ وموجٌ.
يتعبُ الضوءُ الذي في البرجِ.
يتعبُ الرأسُ كثيراً ..
فيميل
آه هلِ تكفي ذراعي ليناموا،
ثُمَّ هلِ تكفي ذراعي ليناموا .. كلّهم
جيشٌ أحبابي وأعدائي جميعاً
قَبْلَ أنْ يأتي نشيشُ الثلج.

*All of Them*


The girl behind the frame tires,
the girl who sweeps the courtyard tires
of the bedlam of marriage,
the girl in the heart tires,
the girl I kissed ten years ago in the darkness
of the roundabout tires,
the girl, who sang at the crossroad
        "We're apart now, O wolf, be thrilled now"
and didn't understand the poem
I wrote for her, tires

The poem that comes walking from the countryside tires,
the one who returns from his illusions alive
with bells and waves in his eyes tires,
the light in the tower tires
and the head tires often then leans . . .
Ah, is my arm enough for them to sleep on?
Is my arm enough for all of them, for the army
        of my loved ones
        and my enemies' army
before whispering snow comes?

عمر

أكادُ أراه
دون أن ألتفت.
زورقٌ مائلٌ للغياب
خيالان في لبن الفجر
مجرى ثقيل وَعشب تَطاولَ فوق المياه.
سينتصفُ النهرُ عمّا قليل
ويشتدُّ صوتُ المجاذيف.
لماذا، إذاً
لا يغنّي الخيالان في لبن الفجر.
لماذا، إذاً، يصمتان
وإلاّ المجاذيف تطعنُ جنيّةَ الماءِ في خصرها
بانتظامٍ ويُسر.

## A Lifetime

I can almost see it
without turning:
a boat leaning
toward absence,
two shadows in dawn's milk,
a slow heavy stream and water grass

The river will soon reach its center,
the paddles will lap louder,
but why
don't the two shadows sing in dawn's milk
why do they keep quiet?

Or do the paddles stab
the water genie
in her waist, rhythmically
and with ease?

## فيما بَعْدُ

في اللّيل،
بعدَ رَحيلهم عنّا
سنجلسُ هادئين، ولن نشدَّ سوى ثيابِ الشرق.
لن نبكي كما يتهيّأ الأوغاد
لن نُلقي على المرآة منديلَ الرماد
ولن نلوّحَ للسنين العَاديات، تمرُّ تحتَ نوافذ العزّاب
فائرة بماءِ الشوق.


بعد رَحيلهم عنّا
سأقسمُ حبّةَ الدرّاق، فرحاناً، إلى قسمين
وأفتحُ دُرْجَ طاولتي
لأخرِجَ ملمسَ السجّاد.

## Later On

at night
after they depart from us
we will sit calmly and will only
pull at the clothes of the east

We won't cry as the bastards think
won't cover our mirrors with handkerchiefs of ash
won't wave to the passing years that stroll by
under the windows of bachelors
         won't bubble with longing's water
after they depart from us
         I will happily split a peach in two
open my desk drawer
and get out that piece of felt

## طيرُ الجنّ

من ثلاثين سنة
وأَنا أَقرأُ في نفس الكتاب
أيقظوني
إنني أحلم بالموت
وأبكي في منامي
آنَ أَنْ أخرج من بهوِ المرايا
آنَ أَنْ أُبصر قلبي
أَنْ أُنادي قوسه العالي ونمضي
كشقيقين
بعيداً عن مساء المئذنة.
ثم لي أن أصرخُ الآن كطيرِ الجنّ
من قلب الخراب
إنه يهتزُّ
عنق السوسنة.

## Jinn Bird

For thirty years
I've been reading the same book,
wake me up
I'm dreaming of death
I cry in my sleep,
it's time I left the hall of mirrors
it's time I saw my heart
and called out to its high arc
so we can move on
as two siblings
away from the evening's minaret,
it's time I screamed like a jinn bird
out of the heart of ruins,
the iris stem
is shaking

منذ سبعة أيام
كان عصر الخميس
قرأت القصيدة
تلك التي ينبغي أن تكون قد اكتملت في الصباح
لم تكن كاملة.

منذ سبعة أعوام
أكملها في الصباح وأغفو
ولكنني حين يأتي المساء
أفاجئها دائماً
وهي تفتح أبوابها خلسة
وتُنادي الكلام.

*Always*

Seven days ago
was Thursday afternoon
I read the poem
the one that was supposed to have been finished
that morning
and it wasn't finished

For seven years
I finish it every morning then doze off
and by evening
I always catch it
opening its doors on the sly
and calling talk in

from

*Not for My Sake*

1992

لَيْسَ مِنْ أَجْلِي

لَيْسَ مِنْ أَجْلِي
ولا من أَجْلِكُم
لَيْسَ من أَجْلِ ما اتّفق الآخرون على وصفهِ
وانتهُوا
الكلام وأحماله
لَيْسَ لي
كلّه كان قبلي.

*Not for My Sake*


Not for my sake
or yours
and not for the sake of what others had agreed to describe
     and fully did
speech and its loads
are not mine
before me
     all of it was

يا بنتُ .. لا تَثقي بنَا
نَبكي ونَضحَكُ
كالملائكة التي هبطتْ، بلا معنى، من الفردوس
واتّكَأَت هُنَا .


نَمشي ونَحكي
والحروبُ وراءنا تعوي، تهشّ صغارها،
وتلمُّ زينتها ...
وتتكسرُ الحراب وتسقط الصيحات خلفَ ظهورنا
وعلى المفارق ينتفُ الأعداءُ ريشَ دعائهم ..
ويُبعثرون الأرض فوق حجارة الطرقات ...
مذهُولين
حين نمرُّ عَبر حصارهم مُترنّحين من النجاة
وصاخبين كما يليق
هواءنا خمر
ومقصدنا الحياة
نمرُّ .. لا نأتي .. ولا نمضي
... ويختلفُ الرّواة.


يا بنتُ ...
لا تثقي بنا
طرقٌ سنسلكها مهيّأة لنا
من أوّل الدنيا أُعدَّ ترابها ... وخطابها
من أوّل الدنيا أُعدَّ الميّتُون بها
وأجراس لها، لو تسمعين،
ترنُّ كي يتوضّأ القتلى
وكي يتفرّق الأحياء في المرآة، تحت السيف
... ثمّ حُروبنا، تلك التي في السهل
ننفلها كما شئنا
ونجلس .. كي تجفّ.
يَا بنتُ لا تَثقي بَنَا
مَنْ سَوفَ يسمعنا ...
سَينسَى عمرهُ
وجناحهُ

*In Praise of Exile*


Girl
don't trust us
we laugh and cry
like angels that have descended from paradise without meaning
and leaned on here

We walk and talk
as wars behind us howl, shoo their young
and gather their accessories, and as spears break
and cries fall behind our backs

And when our enemies
pluck the feathers of their prayers at crossroads
and scatter the earth over pebble paths,
astonished we pass
through their siege
wobbling from the intoxication of survival boisterous as can be:
our air a liquor
our goal a life
we pass without coming or going
as the narrators differ

Girl
don't trust us,
the roads we traverse have been prepared for us
since the beginning of the world:
their dirt, their speeches, their dead
have all been prepared for us, and their bells
if you could hear them ring
for the dead to get up for ablution, also ring
for the living to disperse in mirrors and to the sword

As for our wars, those in the plains, we scatter them as we please
then sit around, wait for them to dry

وبنيه
ثم يهيمُ
حتى نصطفيه

ونحن لا نعد المكان بغير ليلتنا
ولا نعد «الجماعة» بالصلاة.

حيث كنا .. لنا

البيوتُ الصغيرة والأصدقاء الحيارى بأوقاتهم
النساءُ بأكتافهنّ السعيدة والنوم في شُرفات الكلام
طيورُ الغياب  وزهر النميمة
تَعتَعَة السُّكر والضحك في غرف الآخرين
الحُروبُ الأليفة والقادة الطيبُون
يهشّون أحلامنا بالحديد المطاوع والأغبياء،
الشبابُ المليئون بالخير والشرِّ والعافية
... وما لم أعد أذكر الآن.

أنتَ يا صاحبي ضحكة مرّة في جدار البكاء
أنت يا بنتُ ...
غيّرتنا حين ملت
وغيّرتنا حين ملنَا.
والصوَرُ
والحديث الملفّق في كل شيء وعن كل شيء
ورائحةُ البنّ تغوي الممر .. وما مرّ
والولدُ المغربيّ على ضفّة من هواءٍ وخمر
والرقصُ في غفوة الثوب
أنت؟
أم اَلأربعين التي دلفت خلسة
كي تُحبَّ
وكيما تُحبّ؟.

دائماً .. حيث كنا لنا
دائماً حيث لم ننتصر
نترك الأرض غافية،
والمسنُّون والأبرياء
يُضيئون أرياف أيامهم كي يرونا

Don't trust us, girl,
whoever listens to us
will forget their own life
their wings
their children
and will wander
until we pluck them

We don't promise any place
more than one night
or any collective any prayers
and wherever we are is ours

Wherever we are is ours:
the small houses and friends who are at a loss with their time,
the women of happy shoulders and sleep in the balconies of speech,
the birds of absence, the gossip flowers, the drunkard tremor
and bare laugh, the tame wars and kind leaders
who shoo our dreams with pliant steel and imbeciles,
the young men who are filled with good, evil, and health
and whatever else I can't remember now

You, my friend, are a bitter laugh in the crying wall
and you, girl, you changed us
when you leaned this way
and when we leaned along

And the photos,
the made-up chatter about everything and anything,
the smell of coffee as it seduces a hallway,
the dancing in a drowsy dress
and you, you
of forty years who snuck in
so she can love
as she wants to love

وكي يهتفوا خلفنا:
يا إلهي ... غجر!

Always
wherever we are is ours,
always wherever we don't win
we leave the earth asleep
as the elderly and the innocent
illuminate their pastoral days to see us
and chant after us
"O God . . . Gypsies!"

# عرش

اذن،
سوف أبقى
وحيدا وغرّا
كسيف من الماء يلمع في الظلّ.

أرتّب أصداف مملكتي للزوال
وحولي ليل
سيزداد
أو سوف يزداد
كي يصبح الملك أنقى.

*Throne*


I will stay then
alone and green
like a sword of water that gleams in shadow

I will prepare my kingdom's seashells for vanishing
while around me night
grows
will grow
for my reign to become pure

خيانة

كان يعلم،
دائما
وأنا أخبّىء كلّما صادفته ﭔ ثنية الكمّين
آثار الحديقة
واتكاءات الترنّح.

وأنا أراه يرتّب الإصغاء، مهتمّا
ويترك مدية ﭔ المقعد الخالي
ويهرم.
ثم ينهض تاركا ثمرا على الكلمات
زهرا غامضا
ليتمّ ضحكته
حرائق روحه
ومروره العالي عن الأشياء،
يعلم
يا الهي
كان يعلم.

## Betrayal

He always could tell,
whenever I ran into him in the trench,
the trace of the garden in me,
my propping up my wobble

I'd watch him arrange his listening
as he set aside his pocketknife
I'd watch him grow older

then he'd stand up and leave
some fruit hanging on the words,
some mysterious blossoms
that help him to complete his laugh
and lift the fires of his soul
above small matters

He knew,
my God, he always knew!

## الذي يُكذب الآن

هَا هُم الأصدقاء
يهبطون الدرج.
يُولِمون الصّدى للذهاب.

هَا هُم الأصدقاء
يتركون المكان خفيفاً على شرشفِ المائدة.

الحيارى العجيبون
والصفوة الأوفياء.
ينقلون كراسيّهم من أمام البيوت
ويمضُون.

والكلام القديم
الكلام المضيء
الذي شدّنا من قرى في عروق الجبال
كخيطِ الدُّخان
الكلامُ العزيز الّذي، والّذي ...والذي،
يكذب الآن.

*That Is Lying Now*


Here they are, friends
coming down the stairs
preparing a feast for echo's departure

Here they are, friends
leaving the place behind, simple on the tablecloth

They, the perplexed and strange
the select and loyal
transfer their chairs that sat in front of houses
and leave

And that old talk
the illuminated talk
that pulled us out of villages in the veins of mountains
like a thread of smoke

that dear talk that
is lying now

ألعابُهم

نامُوا على الشُبَّاك
منذ مساء أمس يُراقبون النوم
ثمة منزل في اللّيل يشرع بابه
لتمرّ نحو بيوتنا خيل النعاس.


وجدوا حريراً في إناءِ الزهر
سوطاً في الكلام.


وجدُوا طيوراً في المنافض
خنجراً في الضوء،
بوقاً تحتَ غليون المدرّس،
ضفدعاً في ضحكة الشرطيّ،
تقفز في الطريق فينعطف.


وجدوا جياداً في هدير الحافلات
وغمزة مخبوءة في آخر المرآة،
ثمّة منزل ...
نعسُوا   فنامُوا.


ثمّ من كل الممرّات أتاني صوتها
تمشي وتضحك في الغُرف.

*Their Toys*

They slept by the windows
they'd been watching sleep since the night before,
there was a house that had cast its doors
wide open for the horses of drowsiness
to pass by our houses

They found silk in the flowerpots,
whips in speech,
birds in feather dusters,
daggers in light,
a trumpet under the teacher's smoking pipe,
a frog in the policeman's laugh
that leaps and causes him to swerve

They found horses in bus engines
and a wink hidden at the end of mirrors

There was a house,
they got sleepy and slept

Then out of each hallway her voice came to me
she was laughing and walking
in the rooms

امرأةٌ في دمشق في تلك السنة

روحُها في يدي
وِهي تعلمُ أنّي هناك
أداوي الكلام
بما ترك الغيم من صُوفه
فوق نوم السطوح.


أرتقي سُلّماً من ثلاثين طوق
النهايات فوق
ونسوتنا الواقفات على أُهَبَةٍ للبُكاءِ
من الشوق.


وِهي تعلم أنّي هناك
أشعِلُ النار كي تهتدي الكائنات إلى قلبها.
أهشُّ الجنادب من عشب مشيتها.


النهار إلى الظلّ
والعصر لليّل
والحافلات البطيئة، ذاكرة الريف، بيت الملاك
على السفح جانحة
بانتظار الهلاك.

## A Woman in Damascus That Year

Her soul's in my hand and she knows I'm there
medicating speech
with the wool that clouds have left behind
on the roof of sleep

I climb a ladder of thirty collars,
endings are up higher
as are the women who stand on the threshold
of longing tears

And she knows I'm there lighting a fire
so creatures can find her heart

I shoo grasshoppers
out of the grass in her stride, day into shadow
and afternoon into night

While slow buses, memories of the countryside,
and the angel's house
are all reclining on slopes
waiting for an end

بينما هي نائمة في بغداد

وجهها نائم منذ وقت
كبرت، ربما، في المنام
كبرت أو بكت.

قلبها لا يُرى
والسماء الصغيرة والنهرُ
والنسوة الواقفات على طرف الحقل
والإخوة الخمسة الغائبُون يُضيئُون من أوّل الذكريات
فنمشي على هَدْيِهم
وَحْدَنا.

اقطفي زهرة
كَيْ نُصدِّق أنّا هُنا.

ثم لمّا نُنادى
بلا سبب
كي نُنادى.
لنمضي إلى حيث لا نستطيع البقاء
ستضحك أجسادنا بعدنا.

بيننا بيتها في الهواء.

يغمق الضوء خلف الستائر
والنهر يغمق
والجسر والنسوة الواقفات سُدى
والرّفوف، الكلام الذي في الطريق إلى الآخرين
الثياب وضحكتها في الهواء.

إذاً
لم يعد عمرها واضحاً،
وحده قلبها كان يبدو
مائلاً وهو يصعد في لوحة الزيت
حيث النساء على طرف الحقل

## While She Was Sleeping in Baghdad

Her face's been asleep for a while
or perhaps she looks older in sleep,
had grown older or had been crying

Her heart doesn't see,
and the little sky, the river, the women
standing on the edge of the field,
and the five absent brothers
flare at the beginning of memories
as we walk that path alone
the two of us:

"Pick a flower!
We may believe we're here

and when we're called
for no reason besides being called
let's go to where

we can't stay
and our bodies, after us, will chuckle"

A flower
and its house in air are
between us

Light darkens behind the curtains,
the river darkens
the bridge, the women stand in vain,
the shelves,
the talk that's on its way to others,
the clothes and her laugh in air

Then her age was no longer clear

والحقل يَذْوي.
حين لا أستطيع البكاء أو الخوف
أروي :
وحدهُ قلبها كان يبدو
والسنون التي تشبه الخيل
تعدُو.

Only her heart appeared
to lean as it climbed the oil painting
where the women on the edge of the field
were and the field was
wilting

And where I cannot cry or fear
I narrate:
Only her heart appeared

and the years
that resembled horses
kept running

### لم نكن هناك

ولـمّا لم نكن في البيت
جاءَ فتى ليلعبَ في الحديقة
كان يسعلُ في الظلال
فتذبل الأوراق فوق قميصه المبتل.


جاءت خمس زهرات من البيت المجاور
وانقطفنَ بلا مناسبة
بلا أحد
فقط
للظلّ.


جاء محمود الذي كتفاه نَاحلتان،
محمود الّذي يبكي
من الحصص الأخيرة والقواعد والحساب ولا يغشّ
وينحني كالخيززرانة في العراك
وفي القصاص وحين يكتب قطعة الإملاء،


محمود الذي قتلته أفعى
حينَ كنّا ننفل الأعشاش قرب «السلط»،
قشٌّ في يديه
وفي خواتم شعره ريش وقشّ.

*We Weren't There*


And when we weren't at the house
a boy came to play in the garden,
coughed in the shadow and the leaves
wilted on his wet shirt

Five flowers from the neighboring house came
and were plucked without reason
by no one
only for shadow

Mahmoud, with the skinny shoulders, came
Mahmoud who used to cry
because of math and classes at day's end
but who never cheated
and used to bend
like a bamboo stalk when in scuffle
or punishment
and while writing

Mahmoud who was killed by a snake bite
when we used to ruffle
nests near Salt

His hand was holding some hay,
his head curls wore straw rings
and bird feathers

## منعُ تجوُّل

نبات السّكوت يعرّش في جنبات القرى
نبات السّكوت الذي لا يُرى
والخُطَى المريَبة
تهوّم في شهقات الظلال.

ونحن نفتّش بين الأكاليل عن موتهم.
بينما يدخل الشهداء إلى صمتهم
كلّ مَمْلَكَةٍ
مَمْلَكَة.

*Curfew*


The foliage of silence trellises the edges of villages
the unseen foliage of silence

and nervous steps nod
in the gasps of shadows as we search
in laurels for their death

while martyrs enter their hush

Every reign
is sovereign

نجاة أيضا

لو أنّي «هناك» كما أراد أبي
ويرغب اخوتي
وأحب.

لو أني هناك
كما أرادت، دائما، أمي
وحاول صاحبي عبثا
وشاء الحزب.

لو أني هناك
أهشّ باب البيت عن زوارنا
وأعدّ ماء العائلة،
لكبرت مثل أقاربي
ولمتّ مثل أبي
وشبت كأصدقائي كلّهم
وحلقت شعري مثلهم
وهلكت ﻲﻓ طقم المدرّس
دون ريب.

## A Survival Also

Were I there as my father had wished
and my brothers had hoped
and as I would love
were I there

as my mother had always wanted
and my best friend had uselessly tried
and the political party that failed
to enlist me
were I there

waving our house doors open
for our guests
and pouring family water

I would grow old as my relatives did
and die as my father died
and turn gray as all my friends turned

I would have their same haircut
and be buried in a teacher's uniform
without doubt

## أشياء لا تحدث

لو وردة تحمي المدينة
لانقطفتُ لها
على قلق
ومهل.

لو موعد يحمي المكان
لخنتهُ
ليظل.

*Things That Don't Happen*


If a rose could protect the story
I would let myself be plucked for it
anxiously
and patiently

If an appointment could protect the place
I'd stand it up
so it could linger

البيت أيضاً

كان قرب المخيم نهر
وفي بيتنا غائبون
وأيدٍ ستوقظنا ذات يوم سُدى.

كنت في أوّل السابعة
بينما كان يجلس في الظلّ
يكوي ملابسه،
المعطف الأزرق المنحني عند كتفيه.

لم أنتبه للطريق
ولا الدرجات الثلاث
ولم أنتبه للبساط
ولم أنتبه
لستُ أذكر من قال في ذلك اليوم ،
لي أو لغيري،
: يصبحُ الشعر بيتك أمّاً كبرت.

الغبار الذي يأكل الذكريات
سيُبعدهم دائماً
ثم تبدو كراسيّهم من بعيد
وراء التلال وفوق البيوت
مُعلّقة في هواء من الصيف والسنديان
مظلّلة وهي تأتي إلى القلب
محمولة
فوقها خمس زهرات.

أيّ الزهور الكلام
وأيّ الزهور السّكوت.

ولا أستطيع التذكُّر
هل كان خالي على الباب
يُومئُ للصِّبْيَة السُّمْر أن يكبُروا.

*Also the House*


Near the camp was a river
and in our house were absentees and hands
that will one day wake us in vain

I had just turned seven
while he was sitting in the shade
ironing his clothes
the blue jacket sagging over his shoulders

I paid no attention to the road
or the three steps
and didn't notice the carpet

I don't remember who was it that said
to me or to another
"When you grow up poetry will become your house"

The dust that eats the memories
always distances those folks

yet their chairs appear from afar,
from behind the hills and over the houses,
to hang in an air of summer and holm oak,
those shaded chairs that reach the heart
on shoulders topped
with five flowers

Which flowers are speech
which flowers are silence?

And I can't remember
whether it was my uncle who stood at the door,
whether we had palm and lotus trees
in our house in Karameh,

النخلُ والسدرُ في دارنا في «الكرامة»
أُمّي التي ولدتني على الرفّ
تطوي ملابسنا خلسة عن أبي
كي يَنام.


الكلابُ التي للحراسة
تبكي من الحرّ.


الشعرُ في دارنا والحسينيّ والخضر
عمّي الذي جاءَ من بركة في جدار الخليل،
ستُخبرنا صورةٌ بعد عشرين عام :
كبرنا إذاً، وانتهى الأمر.


وكانَ أبي يُربكُ الأصدقاء بأيّامه
والنساء بخيط الغواية في صوته،
وهو يُلقي الكلامَ لأنهارهنَ ويمشي هنا أو هناك
مائلاً، كان يمشي، قليلاً
فتسقطُ أيّامه وهو يمشي
وكانوا يلمُّونها خلفه، وهو يمشي على ذهب
جاءَ من أجله وحده.


ثم لا أستطيع التذكُّر
في حوشنا سنديان
وبركة ماء
وأرض مبلّطة قرب باب كبير
ونحن حَيارَى ومستعجلون
الخزانة في الصدر، في الغرفة الثانية
ومرآتها
حيث نسعى إلى الآن.


وكان أبي واقفاً وحده في الممرّ الذي يصعد الدّرجات
إلى السطح
يشكر أيّامه
أو يُعدّ لقيلولة الأربعاء صباح الخميس
ويترك، فيما سيترك، قنّينة الماء والماء فيها
وحول كراسيّه ينهض السبت.

whether my mother
who gave birth to me on the shelf
was folding our clothes behind our father's back
so he could sleep

The watchdogs used to cry from the heat,
and poetry, Husseini of Jerusalem,
and Khidr the mystic were all in our house
as was my uncle who came from a pond
within Hebron's walls

Twenty years would pass before a photo could tell us
we have grown older
and that's that

My father used to discompose his friends
with his days, and women
with the thread of seduction in his voice
as he would sprinkle chatter in their rivers
while walking about here or there with a lilt,
he'd let his days fall off him
and let others gather them as he walked
on gold that came only for him

And I can't remember:
in our courtyard there were holm oaks,
a fountain, a tiled floor by a huge door,
we were confused and in a hurry

The closet that faced us in the second room
had a mirror
the mirror we now seek

And my father was standing alone in the hall that led
the stairs to the roof
thanking his days
or preparing for Wednesday's nap

وكان أبي لا يُريد الكثير من العمر.
بيت وخمسة أولاد
لا يعبثون بأوراقه، وهي فوضى،
وبنتان كيما تطوف الضفائر ﭬي البيت.

or Thursday's morning
as he left, among the things he'd leave, the water can
full of water
while around his chairs our Saturdays rose

My father didn't want too much from life:
a house, five boys
who don't mess with his papers,
which were already chaos,
and two girls
so that braids could float all around the house

from

*Zodiac of the Horse*

1998

بينما أنت في البيت

أنت في البيت
مشغولة أنت لا تنظرين.


سيبدو الممر طويلاً
وتبدو يداك على حافة الرفّ
مهمومتين بأحلام غامضة
ترفعان الكلام إلى فوق.
أعلى كثيراً من الخوف.


كانوا على عجل يكبرون
وأيامهم خلفهم
تتحنّى فوق سجّادة الارتباك.


إذا ما نظرت:
سيبدو ترذّدهم واضحاً في الهواء
وفي قهوة الظهر
أخطاؤهم وهي تذهب.
فيما سيبقى الممرّ طويلاً
وأنت
مبذّدة
تجلسين هناك.


ذاك الصباح، تلك الوسائد

*Three Hallways*

1

You're at home
busy and don't look about you

The hallway will seem long,
your hands at the edge
of the shelf will seem
burdened by mysterious dreams
and will raise speech higher
much higher than fear

They will grow up in a hurry
their days behind them
will prostrate over apprehension's rug

Are you watching

their hesitation
will seem clear in the air
and in noon's coffee,
their errors in exit are clear

But the hallway will remain long
as you
squandered
sit there

## ذاك الصباح

وتلك الوسائد
رائحة البنّ تهوي على مهل تحت قوس الممرّ.

الكلام المبدّد فيه.

الممرّ الذي امتلأ الآن بالغائبين
وبالضوء والظلّ
والانشغال
ورمل التردّد.
حيث مشاة ينادون إخوتهم
حين أكتافهم في الغبار
وأحمالهم، نحن أو غيرنا،
وانحناءاتهم وهي تطوي الممرّ.
وحين الذي في الهواء الغياب
وهمهمة الخائفين.

بكى
كل شيء هنا
بينما أنت
لا تعرفين.

2

That morning
those cushions
the coffee bean scent slowly descending
from the hallway's arch
the squandered talk there
the hallway packed with absentees
with light and shadow
and preoccupations
and the sand of dithering
where marchers call out to their brothers
call with shoulders full of dust
their loads (theirs or ours) in dust
and their bending
that folds the hallway
when what was in the air was absence
and the mutterings
of those who were scared

Everything here cried
while you
didn't know

## الذي لا يهمّ

أنت مشغولة بالذي لا يهمّ.
ماذا فعلت بشمس الثلاثاء.
ماذا فعلت بحقل الخميس،
بنافورة اليوم.

ماذا فعلت بنا،
نحن، حرّاسك الباهتين.

نناديك،
نحلم لمّا تمرّين بالخيل.

نحلم من أجلنا
كي نظل.

نرى ما رأينا
ونحلم ﻓﻲ حلمنا.

حين نغلق ﻓﻲ الليل شبّاكنا المرّ
كنّا نناديك.

يبدو الممرّ بطيئاً هنا
والشبابيك أقسى
وتلمسنا وهي تحبو الظلال
فننعس.

إلاّ لياليك
إلاّ لياليك
ليست لننسى.

3

You're busy with what doesn't matter

What did you do with Tuesday's sun?
What did you do with Thursday's field
or today's fountain?
What did you do with us
your faint guards?

We call you
when you pass on horses,
you dream for our sake
so that you remain able
to see what we saw
and dream what we dreamed

We used to call you
when we shut our windows on bitter nights

But the hallways seem slow here
the windows harsher
and shadows touch us as they creep
and we fall
asleep

Except your nights
your nights
are not for us
to forget

from

*Luring the Mountain*

1999

عودة

كانوا هنا
المواقدُ دافئةٌ
والحريرُ على الأرضِ
..رائحةُ النومِ والقشِّ تُعمي المكان.

صوتُ ارتطامِ النباتاتِ بالخيلِ،
ما ظلَّ..
أو ما يشي بانهمارِ الدفوفْ.

كانوا هنا
الموائدُ مرصوفةٌ للجدارِ
الزجاجاتُ فارغةٌ كلُّها
والكؤوسُ على حالِها..

مثلَ زهرٍ قتيلٍ نما ﰲ الرفوفْ.

*Return*

They weren't here
the kilns are warm
the silk is on the ground
the smell of sleep and hay blind the place

The sounds of plants colliding with horses
and what remains
or betrays the pouring of tambourines

They weren't here
the tables are stacked against the wall
the bottles are all empty
the glasses are as they were

like some murdered flowers that have
sprouted on the shelves

## أعداء

في سفينتهمِ
يهرمُ الصوت
بينما يبصرُ النائمونَ قرابينَ أجدادهم
وهي تمشي على الماء
حيث الروايةُ تقتلُ أولادَها
ثمّ تهبطُ في الليلِ من ظلها
آمين..
آمين
في إثرها
والقرابينُ
والنافخونَ

وفي إثرهم كلّهم
يُولَدُ الزيتُ !

*Enemies*


On their ship
sound grows old
while the sleeping
see their ancestors' offerings walk on water
where the story commits infanticide
then at night descends its own shadow
Amen
Amen
on its trail
along with the offerings
and the trumpeters

And on their tracks
oil is born

الكلب والساعة

كان رتلُ الجنودِ اليهودِ يُنقِّبُ شَعْرَ الهواءِ
ويبحثُ عنّا
وعن أهلِنا في « الكرامة »

كانت تدقُّ !

فيعدو بنا الوقتُ
حتى الضواحي القريبةِ « للسلطِ »
والنهر.

ساعتنا تلكَ
فوق الخزانةِ
في بيتِنا
في « الكرامة » .

كان النباحُ يحاولُ أن يفتحَ البابَ من أوَّلِ الليل
كان الركامُ على الأرضِ حيثُ انتهى بيتُنا والخزانة
والنخلتانِ وكلبُ الحراسةِ واللوحُ في غرفةِ الصفِّ والصفّ.

كانت تدقُّ

وكان النباحُ المنقَّطُ يسقطُ من فروةِ الكلبِ
فوق الممرِّ
وفوق الوسائدِ
والنوم
والشأيِ والزيتِ
والساعةِ الخامسة.

*The Dog and the Clock*


A file of Jewish soldiers was combing the air's hair
looking for us
and for our family in Karameh

It was ticking
          and time took us running
to the nearby suburbs of Salt and to the river

That clock of ours
above the closet
in our house
in Karameh

The barking was trying to open the door early at night
and where our house and closet end
rubble was on the ground
the two palm trees
          the watchdog
                    the chalkboard in the classroom
                              and the classroom

It was ticking
          while the spotted barking fell from the dog's fur
in the hallway
on the pillows
over sleep
into tea and oil
and five o'clock

ترنيمة النائم

أصعدُ النومَ
أدراجُهُ سبعةٌ،
أنت ﻓﻲ النوم
مرثيّةُ الذاهبَاتِ
وايقونةُ اللوم.

أصعدُ النومَ
أدراجُهُ سبعةٌ
بالتمامْ.

ولا يحدثُ الأمرُ
أو ينتهي.

أُشعلُ الضوءَ
كي يبصرَ الميّتونَ المنام.

## The Sleeper's Hymn

I climb sleep
its seven steps
you're in sleep
an elegy of the gone
and censure's icon

I climb sleep
its seven steps
exactly seven

and it doesn't happen
or it ends

I turn the light on
for the dead to see
what sleep is

ترنيمة المنفي

لا أناديك زلفى
ولا اهتدي عنوةً
انّ لي نبأً في ثنايا الكلامِ
ومنفايَ
منفى.
لم يقل ذاكَ يوماً
ولمْ ..
كان يَغرفُهُ
مثل ماءٍ
وينساهُ
بينما يشربُ العابرونَ
ويدعون للبئرِ.
مرّتْ ثلاثُ يمامات
في ميلة العصرِ
صقرٌ وأنثاه
اسماؤهنّ جميعاً، خطاياهُ أو أهلُهُ
والترددُ
كان الترددُ ينهالُ أبيضَ من غابةٍ
في الجوار العميقِ
الذي لا يَراه
حيثُ ينبعُ منفاه.

## Exile's Hymn

Unlike a sycophant I call to you
uncoerced I find my way to you
I have news
in the folds of speech
and my exile
is exile

He never said that
and never . . .
He used to scoop it up
like water
then forget it

while passersby would drink
and pray to the well

Three doves flew by
in afternoon's slope,
a male hawk, a female hawk,
all their names, his sins or his kin
and hesitation

Hesitation was pouring white from a forest
in the nearby depth that he couldn't see . . .

where his exile springs

# ترنيمة الممَر

المَمَرُّ المرتَّبُ في صوتِها
للكلامِ الصغير.

الممرُّ الذي يكسرُ النومَ
كيما يسيلِ المنام.

سوفَ تُهْملُنا وردةٌ فيه
زنبقةٌ ، ربَّما

حينَ تَبِشُ جارَتُنا نومَها كلَّهُ
كي ترانا هنا في الكلام
أوتفكِّرَ بالشام.

لَيْتَها أُخْتُنا
أو هي الآن.

## The Hallway's Hymn

The hallway in her voice is tidy
for small talk

the hallway that breaks sleep in order
for sleep to flow

is where a rose will neglect us
or an iris perhaps

is when our neighbor snatches all our sleep
to see us here in speech
or to think of Syria

I wish she were our sister
or she is now

## ترنيمة المشتاق

بَيْتُها
بَيْتُها!
والزجاجُ المُعشَّقُ في بيتِها
في دمشقَ
والنسوةُ الحائراتُ من الهجرِ
والصبرِ
والشوقِّ.

والآخرونَ الذينَ على ظلِّها يَحُدّثونَ
كما فوقَ سُرَّتِها يحدثُ الثوب.

الرضى والندامة
والبحثُ عن نيّة للسلامة
كالنومِ في نومِها دون ذنب.

صوتُها
صوتُها!

حيثُ يأتي الكلامُ على مهلهِ كي
يرى.

## Hymn for Longing

Her house
is her house

and the dovetailed glass in her house
in Damascus
and the women perplexed by abandonment
patience
and longing

And the others who happen on her shadow
as a dress happens on her navel

Satisfaction and regret
and the search for a meaning to safety
like sleeping in her sleep without guilt

Her voice
is her voice

when speech slowly arrives in order
to see

*أغنية العاشق*


أنت لا تعرفينَ
كلَّ يوم أزورك في الليل
أروي عَليك مَنامي الأَخير
وَنَجلسُ حتى يجفُّ الكلامُ.


ونبقى على حالنا تلكَ
ظلَّين في الظلِّ.


ليستْ لنا الأغنية
وليستْ لنا النارُ في السهل
ثمّةَ من يحرسُ الميتينَ هناك.

*The Lover's Song*


You have no clue
I visit you every night
to tell you my latest dream

Together we sit
until talk dries up then we remain
two shadows in shadow

The song isn't ours
the fire in the plains not ours,
someone's guarding the dead there

## أغنية الغريب

كان الندى ﰲ البلاد الغريبة يبكي على الباب
كانت ضفافُ الدروب تسوقُ المهارى الى الموت
كان المكانُ نظيفاً بأوصافه العشر
كان الثوابُ على الأرض حَيثُ انتَهى كلُّ وقتٍ به

والمحبُّونَ والأدعياءُ
وما تركَ الأولياءُ
من الخبزِ فوقَ الدعاء
معي.

أيُّ أمرٍ سَيغويكَ عَنِّي !

كان طيرُ الكلامِ البطيء، صباحَكَ
يرمي شعائرَهُ ﰲ الضحى
كان ﰲ القلبِ نومٌ سيأوي الى ريفِه كي ينام.

وشيءٌ من العمرِ ﰲ ظاهرِ الكفِّ
يروي
وينسى.

الوجوهُ التي ذهبتْ لم تزلْ ﰲ خيوطِ الهواء
الدروبُ لها صوتها
، لو عرفتَ،
وما زال للتبغ طعمُ التمنّي
وللقادمين مَرايا الغياب.

رأى
واشتهى

وانتهى
السرُّ
فارفعْ هواءَك
زوّارُ بيتكَ غاوون
أوصافُهم ﰲ الكتاب.

## The Stranger's Song

In strange countries dew was crying at the door
and roadsides drove colts to death

The place with its ten attributes was clean,
reward on earth was where each time ends

And lovers and evangelists
and what saints leave behind
of prayers and breads
were with me

What will lure you away from me?

Your morning, that bird of slow talk
tossed its rituals to dusk,
and some sleep in the heart was heading to its countryside
to sleep

And something of life on the back of the hand
was narrating
forgetting

If only you knew
that the faces that went would remain in threads of air,
if only you knew that the paths would each have a voice,
tobacco would have the taste of a wish
and newcomers would have the mirrors of absence

He saw and desired
and it was done

The secret
was done
so lift your air

محبُّكَ
ما نام شبّاكهُ
أو سها .

your house visitors are a bunch of tempters
their attributes are in the book

Your lover's window
has not slept
or overlooked you

أغنية المفقود

فرادى في الممرِّ رأيتُهم
وسمعتُ صيحتَهم
فرادى
وانتظرتُ
كرمية في الظلِّ
أحلمُ بالهواءِ
ممزَّقاً
لِمَ
لِّمَ
أنادَ.

*Song of the Missing*


One by one in the hallways
I saw them
heard their hollering
one by one
and waited
like a fling in shadow
dreaming of air
ripped
air
why
why didn't I
shout

أغنية الدوريات الثلاث

لم نجيءٌ بالنجوم
لم نجيءٌ بالنبيذ
لم نجيءٌ بالصَدَفْ.

لم نكنْ في السماء
لم نكنْ في الكروم
ولم نقطف البحر.

هل صدَّقَ الريفُ حقّاً
وهل صدَّقت أمُّنا
أنَّهُ ينقطف.

## Song of the Three Patrols

We didn't come bearing stars
we didn't come bearing wine
we didn't come bearing seashells

We weren't in the sky
we weren't in vineyards
and didn't harvest the sea

Did the countryside really believe
and did our mother also believe
that it can be harvested?

## صوت

مضى العمرُ
لا قطفَ القلبُ لوزَ الشتاء
ولا هبَّ ﻹ الروح سيفُ اَلرضى.

مضى العمرُ
حيّا جدائلنا
وانقضى.

على عجلٍ هزَّ كوكَبهُ وانشى.

مضى العمرُ
لا
تتركيني
هنا.

## A Voice

Life passed
without the heart
picking the almonds of praise,
without the sword
of content rising in the soul

Life passed
it greeted our braids
and ended

in a hurry
it shook its planet and bent

Life passed
don't
leave me here

أبناء النخل

مرّوا علينا
في العشّية أو على أطرافِها
خُطّارُ بيد
أنجبتْهُم نَخلةٌ
ورمتْ بهم للوقت
تلك بلادُكم، قالت،
وقد مكثْتَ هناك
فساكنوها أشهراً حتى تلين
وغادروا ليلاً
ولا ترثوا هنا.

مرّوا علينا
يكشفونَ السرَّ والرؤيا
ولا يتعجّلونَ الأمرَ
هون مشيُهم
وحديثُهم شجن.

لسنا على عجل
شربنا من فراتٍ
وانتَظَرْنا
أطعَمَتْنا مرأةٌ تمراً
وقبّلت الصغيرَ على محبّتنا
وأوصتْنا به خيراً
وأوصتْنا
بنا.

## Children of Palm Trees

At evening they passed us by
or by the evening's outskirts they passed us by
a bunch of desert pendulums
born to a palm tree
that chucked them to time
      and said, That's your land
      it's been there
      cohabitate
      with it until it softens
      then leave at night
      and bequeath nothing here

They passed us by
exposing secret and vision
never in a rush
their gait easy
their conversation sad:
      We're not in a hurry
      we drank from the Euphrates
      and waited
      a woman fed us dates
      kissed our young for loving us
      entrusted them to us
      and us
      to us

from

*Biography in Charcoal*

2003

# أعمى

أين تمضي
حين تنطفئُ الدورُ
الطرق.

حين أمشي
مثل تلويحٍ من الماضي
وحيداً في هسيسِ الأربعين.

أين أمضي
حينما أخرجُ من أيقونةِ الذكرى
وقد نوديت
في أرضٍ من الجان

سعيداً
هائماً كالصوتِ
أو
أعمى
يدبُّ على المكان!

## Blind

Where do you go
when houses when roads
put their lights out

when I walk
like a gesture from the past
alone in the whispering at forty

Where do I go
when I exit memory's icon
when summoned
in a land of jinn
happy

or wandering like a sound
or a blind man
creeping about the place

اتبع الرائحة

اتبع الرائحة يا ضبع
اتبع الرائحة.

اتبعها وحيداً، مرقّطا، هائما
كأنّكَ لا تدري
واضْحك في وديان وعرة
يَشحب صخرُها ويَسوَدّ.

اتبعها يا ضبع.
اتبعْ قتّاليك حتى نوافذهم المنخفضة
واعبر بسراجَيك نومتهُم
وبدّل برائحتك أجسادَهُم.
ادفعهم إلى الليل بلطف حيلتك
دائخينَ، يتعثّرون في أحلامهم.

اتبع الرائحة يا ضبعُ
يا أبانا
الضاحكَ
في
الوديان.

## Follow That Smell

Follow that smell, hyena
follow that smell
alone and spotted and roving
as if you didn't know

and laugh in rugged valleys
whose rocks are sallow then black

Follow it, hyena
follow your murderers to their low windows
and with your two lanterns pass through their sleep,
exchange their bodies with your scent

With their placid trickery push them toward the night
dizzy and stumbling in their slumber

Follow that smell, hyena
you laughing
father
      of ours
           in the valleys

## الكرامة ١٩٦٥

الهديرُ الذي كان يصعد منذ الطفولةِ
من جهة النهر،
حيث التلالُ ستهبط للماء لمّا ننام،
وحيث الحقول ستنهض في الليلِ بعد العشاء
وتصعد للدير.

الهديرُ الذي كنتُ أسمعهُ، غامضاً،
وهو يصعدُ نحو «الكرامة» و«السلط»،
حيث الكلابُ التي نبحت دون جدوى.

الهدير الذي كان يذرع تلك النواحي
ويزحف تحت المصاطبِ والدور والقشّ.

يتبعني من جديدٍ.

نحنُ في تونسَ الآن
والخيلِ تعدو إلى حجر الأربعين
ومن أولِ العمر، أقصَى التذكر
تنبحُ تلك الكلابُ العنيدةُ في الحوش.

## Karameh 1965

The ripple that kept rising since childhood
from the direction of the river

where the hills come down to the water when we sleep
where the fields get up at night after dinner
and climb to the convent

the ripple I used to hear, mysterious, as it climbed
toward Karameh and Salt
where the dogs barked to no avail

the ripple that used to stroll those corners
and crawl under planks, houses, and hay

is following me again . . .

We are now in Tunis
and horses
are galloping toward the rock

of forty years
while in the remotest memory
those stubborn dogs bark in the courtyard

دمشق ١٩٨٦

لم تكن لي رنّةُ المفتاح
والشمسُ التي ناديتها من درفة الشباك
والوقت القليل من المودّة.

ليس لي هذا الصباح الضيّق
المرشوش فوق حديقة الجيران
من طرف المخدّة.

لم تكن لي
ضحكةُ البنت التي لمعت وراءَ المزهرية
في الهواء.

لا بدّ أنَّ يدا تقطّف ياسمينا في الجوار.

لو تغلقُ المذياعَ، جارتُنا، فأسمع
كيفَ تتكسر المياه على يديها وهي تغسل.

كنتُ سأفتح الشبّاك
كنتُ سأطفئ الأضواء.

*Damascus 1986*


The key's clang
the sun I called from the windowsill
the brief time of fondness
none of it was mine

This cramped morning
sprinkled over the neighbor's garden
from the edge of the pillow
isn't mine

It wasn't mine
that laugh of the girl who gleamed behind the vase
in air

There had to be a hand picking jasmine nearby

If only our neighbor would turn off the radio
I could hear
how water breaks over her hands as she washes . . .

I would have opened the window
I would have turned off the lights

ها هو البيت
واجهةٌ من زجاج
وبوابةٌ من قصبٍ.

عتمةٌ في الممرِّ
وليمونةٌ أزهرتْ منذُ يومين
لوزٌ على الجانبين
و«نارجيلة» دون ماء
ستبصرنا حالما نفتح الباب نحن الثلاثة

ظلُّ الحديقةِ يمشي
ورائي
ورائحة الياسمين.

سأجلسُ حيثُ تعوّدتُ
ظلُّ الحديقة فوقَ البساط
ورائحةُ الياسمينِ على الثوب

ثوبٌ من الصيف ،
من أولِ الصيف،
ثوبُ الفتاةِ التي لم أحبَّ.

*Tunis 1992*

Here is the house
a glass front
and a reed door

A darkness in the corridor
a lemon that has just blossomed
two days ago

Almond trees on both sides
a waterless hookah will spot us
as soon as the three of us enter

The garden's shadow walks
behind me and the jasmine scent

I'll sit where I used to sit
the garden's shadow over the mat
the jasmine smell on a dress

A summer dress
early summer
the dress of the girl I didn't love

ولدٌ بكّاء
ابنُ جارتنا المسيحية
يكسرُ غصنَ الهدهدِ على الصنوبرةِ
وييكي..
قشّاتٌ خفيفةٌ
تطير في إثرهِ وتلسعُه.

ريشٌ ونحلٌ وطيورٌ في إثرهِ
وهو يركضُ تحتَ النافذة.
صنوبرةٌ معوّجة تتبعه.
والولدُ يركضُ نحو الشارعِ
وييكي...
والبكاءُ يحيطُ به
ويدفعه

والولد البكّاء يركضُ نحوَ الخرائبِ..
.. بينما
أفعى الخرائبِ، ذاتُ الأجراسِ،
تنصت، متيقظةً،
لكلِّ هذا
في بئرِ الزيت.

*Birzeit 1998*

A crying boy
that boy of our Christian neighbor's
he'd break the hoopoe's branch on a pine tree
then cry

Hay needles
fly after him and sting him
feathers and birds and bees

are after him
as he runs under the window

a crooked pine tree
follows him

and the boy is running
toward the street
and crying
crying
surrounds him
and propels him

and the crying boy is running
toward the junkyards

while the junkyard snake, the rattling kind,
hearkens, alert
to all of this
in Birzeit

صيحة فوق الحرش

في العتمة متسعٌ
ليد سوداءَ
بخمسٍ أصابعَ
وذراع.

في العتمة بيت
منهمكٌ بمشاغل موتاه
المنهمكين
بنقل نواياهمْ
في القوس.

في العتمة أصواتٌ هلكتْ
وصراخٌ ظلّ على الأحجارِ
وأسيجة القرّاصِ
وماء الحوشِ.

ومثل لحاء خشن تبدو الصيحةُ
فوقَ الحرشِ.

في العَتْمة
حيثُ يحومُ الماضي
حولَ السلّمِ
منطوياً
كقميص باردٌ.

تتعثّرُ أفئدة الموتى
وحفيفُ تجوّلهم في الطرقة
يبدو مثلَ نبات غائر
أو عينين موافقتين تماما.
يمضي السلّمُ متكئًا ووحيدا
نحو بياض تضمرهُ الأقواس.

لا وقتَ ليكفيهمْ
لا وقتَ، ومخذولين

## A Scream over the Woods

In the dark there's room
for a black hand
with five fingers
and an arm

In the dark a house is consumed
with the chores of its dead
who are consumed
with transferring their intentions
to the arch

In the dark ruined voices, screams
that remained on rocks
and in nettle fences
and in the courtyard's water

Like rough bark
a scream appears over the woods

In the dark
where the past roams around the ladder
folded like a cold shirt
the hearts of the dead stumble

and the rustle
of their stroll in the hallway
is like a blind plant
or a pair of consenting eyes

The ladder goes on
leaning alone toward a whiteness
the arches diminish

نواياهمْ معهم، بيضاء،
وعزلتهمْ
فيهم.

من فكّر فينا كي ننهض في العتمة،
ملدوغين بصورتنا
بيضا من أثر النومِ
وثمّة أقواسٌ تتفرّق منّا
شاحبة تبهت في الردهات.

من فكّر فينا، نحن المنسيّين،
ذهبنا في العربات إلى المنفى
ورجعنا
منسيّين
بلا عربات.

and no time is enough for them
no time
and let down
they hold their intentions white

their solitude
within them . . .

Did we cross someone's mind
before we rose in the dark
stung with our image
white from sleep's effect

while arches branched out of us haggard
and grew faint in the hallways?

Who thought of us?
we the forgotten who
boarded vehicles to exile and returned

forgotten
without vehicles

## عربيات في العتمة

لن يبصرَ طرّاقُ الليل يدا
ستؤشّرُ نحوَ جنوب مَنخفض في الظلّ،
طريقا من أكفان بيض
وحصائرَ زرقاءَ.

أيقظ أبناءَك يا أبتي
واتركْ كتفيكَ المائلتين على الشبّاك.

لمشيكَ في جنبات الصيف
حفيفٌ من أسف غلّاب.

أيقظ أبناءك
سوفَ يميلُ الحلمُ بهم
وسينقرُ دفّ
في العاشرة تماما
في المنحدر
ويصعد من أقصاه المعتم
رفّ ذئاب.

## Vehicles in the Dark

The night traveler won't see a hand
that points to a low south in the shadow
or a road of white shrouds and blue mats

Dad, wake your children up and leave
your slanted shoulders by the window,
your gait on the flanks of summer
has a rustle of awesome sorrow

Wake your children up, Dad, dream
will sway with them, a tambourine
will tap down the slope
at exactly ten o'clock

And a pack of wolves
will ascend its far dark edge

# Index of Titles

## About the Author and Translator

Beit Jala–born GHASSAN ZAQTAN is a novelist, editor, and the author of more than ten collections of poetry. His books have been translated into various languages. He was twice nominated for the Neustadt International Prize. *Like a Straw Bird It Follows Me,* the first book of his work to appear in English, received the Griffin International Poetry Prize in 2013. He lives in Ramallah.

FADY JOUDAH is a practicing physician and the author of three collections of poetry and several volumes of poetry in translation from the Arabic. His debut poetry book won the Yale Series of Younger Poets competition, and he has received a Guggenheim Fellowship as well as several awards for translation. He lives in Houston.

# Lannan Literary Selections

For two decades Lannan Foundation has supported the publication and distribution of exceptional literary works. Copper Canyon Press gratefully acknowledges their support.

### LANNAN LITERARY SELECTIONS 2017

John Freeman, *Maps*

Rachel McKibbens, *blud*

W. S. Merwin, *The Lice*

Javier Zamora, *Unaccompanied*

Ghassan Zaqtan (translated by Fady Joudah), *The Silence That Remains*

### RECENT LANNAN LITERARY SELECTIONS FROM COPPER CANYON PRESS

Josh Bell, *Alamo Theory*

Mark Bibbins, *They Don't Kill You Because They're Hungry, They Kill You Because They're Full*

Malachi Black, *Storm Toward Morning*

Marianne Boruch, *Cadaver, Speak*

Jericho Brown, *The New Testament*

Olena Kalytiak Davis, *The Poem She Didn't Write and Other Poems*

Michael Dickman, *Green Migraine*

Deborah Landau, *The Uses of the Body*

Sarah Lindsay, *Debt to the Bone-Eating Snotflower*

Maurice Manning, *One Man's Dark*

Camille Rankine, *Incorrect Merciful Impulses*

Roger Reeves, *King Me*

Paisley Rekdal, *Imaginary Vessels*

Brenda Shaughnessy, *So Much Synth*

Richard Siken, *War of the Foxes*

Frank Stanford, *What About This: Collected Poems of Frank Stanford*

Ocean Vuong, *Night Sky with Exit Wounds*

For a complete list of Lannan Literary Selections from Copper Canyon Press, please visit Partners on our website: www.coppercanyonpress.org

Poetry is vital to language and living. Since 1972, Copper Canyon Press has published extraordinary poetry from around the world to engage the imaginations and intellects of readers, writers, booksellers, librarians, teachers, students, and donors.

**WE ARE GRATEFUL FOR THE MAJOR SUPPORT PROVIDED BY:**

THE PAUL G. ALLEN
FAMILY FOUNDATION

Anonymous

Jill Baker and Jeffrey Bishop

Donna and Matt Bellew

John Branch

Diana Broze

Sarah and Tim Cavanaugh

Janet and Les Cox

Mimi Gardner Gates

Linda Gerrard and Walter Parsons

Gull Industries, Inc.
on behalf of Ruth and William True

The Trust of Warren A. Gummow

Steven Myron Holl

Phil Kovacevich and Eric Wechsler

Lakeside Industries, Inc.
on behalf of Jeanne Marie Lee

TO LEARN MORE ABOUT UNDERWRITING
COPPER CANYON PRESS TITLES,
PLEASE CALL 360-385-4925 EXT. 103

WE ARE GRATEFUL FOR THE MAJOR SUPPORT PROVIDED BY:

Maureen Lee and Mark Busto

Rhoady Lee and Alan Gartenhaus

Ellie Mathews and Carl Youngmann as The North Press

Anne O'Donnell and John Phillips

Petunia Charitable Fund and advisor Elizabeth Hebert

Suzie Rapp and Mark Hamilton

Joseph C. Roberts

Jill and Bill Ruckelshaus

Cynthia Lovelace Sears and Frank Buxton

Kim and Jeff Seely

Catherine Eaton Skinner and David Skinner

Dan Waggoner

Austin Walters

Barbara and Charles Wright

The dedicated interns and faithful volunteers
of Copper Canyon Press

The Chinese character for poetry is made up of two parts: "word"
and "temple." It also serves as pressmark for Copper Canyon Press.

This book is set in Farnham Text with Arabic set in Musa.
Book design by VJB/Scribe with Arabic typography by Aissa Deebi.
Printed on archival-quality paper.